UNITE History
Volume 5 (1974–1992)

The Transport and General Workers' Union (TGWU):
From Zenith to Nadir?

UNITE History
Volume 5
(1974–1992)

The Transport and
General Workers' Union (TGWU):
From Zenith to Nadir?

Mary Davis

LIVERPOOL UNIVERSITY PRESS

First published 2023 by
Liverpool University Press
4 Cambridge Street
Liverpool
L69 7ZU

British Library Cataloguing-in-Publication data
A British Library CIP record is available

ISBN 978-1-80207-850-3

Typeset by Carnegie Book Production, Lancaster
Printed and bound by CPI Group (UK) Ltd, Croydon CR0 4YY

Contents

Figures

Boxes

Acknowledgements

Grateful thanks are due to the regional teams of the UNITE History Project: women and men trade union activists past and present who have contributed to this volume and this unique and ambitious project. This, the fifth of a six-volume history, has been supplemented by local research and oral histories. It is a history of the labour movement for the labour movement. Today's trade unionists, especially those active in UNITE, are the inheritors of past struggles: they have not only a right but a responsibility to reclaim their own past. To paraphrase Marx, we make our own history, even if we do not make it just as we please. As this bleak volume 'From Zenith to Nadir' shows, we do not make it under circumstances chosen by ourselves.

Thanks are also due to the Marx Memorial Library editorial team and to our Advisory Board.

Special thanks to Sol Abrahams for his technological expertise in rendering the graphs and charts readable and decipherable.

Abbreviations

ACAS	Advisory, Conciliation and Arbitration Service
ACTSS	Association of Clerical, Technical and Supervisory Staff
AES	Alternative Economic Strategy
AEU	Amalgamated Engineering Union/Amalgamated Engineering and Electrical Union
APEX	Association of Professional, Executive, Clerical and Computer Staff
ASLEF	Associated Society of Locomotive Steam Enginemen and Firemen
ASTMS	Association of Scientific, Technical and Managerial Staffs
ATGWU	Amalgamated Transport and General Workers' Union (TGWU in Ireland)
AUEW	Amalgamated Union of Engineering Workers
BAME	Black, Asian and Minority Ethnic
BDC	Biennial Delegate Conference
BL	British Leyland
BSC	British Steel Corporation
CBI	Confederation of British Industry
CDRNI	Campaign for Democratic Rights in Northern Ireland
CO	Certification Officer
COHSE	Confederation of Health Service Employees
CPGB	Communist Party of Great Britain
CPRS	Central Policy Review Staff
CPSA	Civil and Public Services Association
CROTUM	Commissioner for the Rights of Trade Union Members
EEC	European Economic Community
EED	Electronics and Engineering Division (Ford Motor Company)
EETPU	Electrical, Electronic, Telecommunications and Plumbing Union

EPA	Employment Protection Act 1975
FBU	Fire Brigades Union
FNJNC	Ford National Joint Negotiating Committee
GEC	General Executive Committee
GLC	Greater London Council
GMWU	General and Municipal Workers Union
GPMU	Graphical Paper and Media Union
HMSO	Her Majesty's Stationery Office
HRM	Human Resource Management
HSWA	Health and Safety at Work Act 1974
ICTU	Irish Congress of Trade Unions
IMF	International Monetary Fund
IT	Industrial Tribunal
JSSC	Joint Shop Stewards Committee
LBL	London Buses Limited
LCDTU	Liaison Committee for the Defence of Trade Unions
LRT	London Regional Transport
LT	London Transport
MRC	Modern Records Centre, University of Warwick
MSC	Manpower Services Commission
MSF	Manufacturing, Science and Finance
NAFF	National Association for Freedom
NALGO	National and Local Government Officers' Association
NAPE	National Association of Port Employers
NAPO	National Association of Probation Officers
NASUWT	National Association of Schoolmasters Union of Women Teachers
NCU	National Communications Union
NDLS	National Dock Labour Scheme
NGA	National Graphical Association
NIC ICTU	Northern Ireland Committee of the Irish Congress of Trade Unions
NILP	Northern Ireland Labour Party
NSCAC	National Steering Committee Against the Cuts
NUDAGMW	National Union of Domestic Appliance and General Metal Workers
NUJ	National Union of Journalists
NUM	National Union of Mineworkers
NUPE	National Union of Public Employees
NUR	National Union of Railwaymen
NUS	National Union of Seamen
NUSWCH&DE	National Union of Sheet Metal Workers, Coppersmiths, Heating & Domestic Engineers
NUT	National Union of Teachers
NWAC	National Women's Advisory Committee

ONS	Office for National Statistics
OPO	one-person operation
PCS	Public and Commercial Services Union
PLA	Port of London Authority
RCN	Royal College of Nursing
RDWs	registered dock workers
RTC	Road Transport (Commercial)
RWAC	Regional Women's Advisory Committee
RWO	Regional Women's Organiser
SERTUC	South East Region TUC
SOGAT	Society of Graphical and Allied Trades
SPG	Special Patrol Group
STUC	Scottish Trades Union Congress
TASS	Technical, Administrative and Supervisory Section
TGWU	Transport and General Workers' Union
TNA	The National Archives, Kew
TUC	Trades Union Congress
UCS	Upper Clyde Shipbuilders
UCW	Union of Communication Workers
UWC	Unemployed Workers' Centre

Foreword

Unite History Project
The Six-Volume History

2022 marks the centenary of the formation of the Transport & General Workers' Union (T&G), now a part of Unite, Britain and Ireland's largest union in private industry. The T&G was also a significant workers' organisation in public sector employment, a tradition carried forward into Unite.

The T&G was the first general trade union, taking pride in organising workers in every occupation and delivering collective bargaining across a multitude of industries. The T&G held real industrial power through much of its history, and it was from this basis that millions of working people won better pay and conditions that dramatically improved living standards.

The union also exercised a great deal of political influence, particularly within the Labour Party. This and its interaction with government, often as a powerful independent actor in its own right, provide the setting for a wider chronological history of the labour movement in Britain – and to that extent also the industrial and political history of Britain; it was not without a significant impact in Ireland as well.

This history reflects and exposes the wider processes of social change in which working people played an active role, in terms of creating an understanding of oppression in society and exploitation, particularly of women and black people, in the workplace. In addition, the union's international work and campaigns are brought into sharp focus.

Many of the T&G's general secretaries, from Bevin to Morris, have been the subject of biographies, and Jack Jones published an autobiography. But this series is different: among other things it examines how the union's central function, campaigning and winning on jobs, pay and conditions, evolved over the course of the twentieth century.

This six-volume series tells this story in a highly original way, as it enables the incorporation of local history as played out by the union's shop stewards and branch officers. Work has been undertaken at regional level, based on interviews and newly uncovered archival material, that brings our history to life and gives a human dimension to an otherwise 'top level' narrative. Unions are after all composed of individuals – in the T&G's case, hundreds of thousands.

I believe that these volumes will make a great contribution to Unite's educational programmes with its members, workplace representatives and other activists, and more generally in colleges and universities; nothing like this work has been published before.

If we are to avoid the mistakes of the past it is of course essential that we understand and learn from it! This series of six books, detailing the history of one of the twentieth century's most important and vital trade unions, gives us that opportunity, and I commend them to you.

Sharon Graham
General Secretary
Unite the Union

Introduction

This volume easily divides itself into two distinct periods. The first, from 1974 to 1979, saw a reforming Labour government, which, recognising trade union strength, was determined to 'bring about a fundamental and irreversible shift in the balance of power and wealth in favour of working people and their families'.[1] The second period, 1979 to 1992, under a right-wing Conservative government led by Margaret Thatcher, was determined to accomplish precisely the opposite. (The distinctive reactions of the Transport and General Workers' Union in Ireland and Scotland to both periods are fully covered in two separate chapters in this volume by John Foster.)

However, trade union strength, and in particular trade union militancy, worried Conservative and Labour governments alike. Both parties, as we have seen in *Unite History*, volume 4, shared a common aim of attempting to reduce union power at shop floor level, and both parties, fixated as they were with reducing both the balance of payments deficit and public spending, attempted to freeze or control wage demands. The two parties, when in government, adopted different methods to accomplish these twin aims, but a key strategy shared by both was a desire to detach the leaderships of trade unions from shop floor militancy. One way of doing this, adopted by the Labour government, was to establish various forms of tripartism – formal and informal meetings between representatives of government, employers and unions, often with the aim of securing agreement on prices and incomes policies in various forms. The desire to achieve such policies (particularly in regard to incomes) dominated government strategic thinking for almost 20 years from 1960 to 1979 but was abruptly halted in the Thatcher years. Another way of curbing trade union effectiveness was to impose legal restrictions on collective

---

1 February 1974 Labour Party manifesto. http://labour-party.org.uk/manifestos/1974/Feb/1974-feb-labour-manifesto.shtml.

bargaining and union action; this route led to serious industrial confrontation, as we have seen in the previous volume, during the late 1960s and the 1970s, and was eventually jettisoned until the Thatcher government successfully reintroduced legal restrictions on union activity.

Political Background, 1974–1992

The 1974 Labour government was elected on a tidal wave of industrial militancy, and for the first time in British history such trade union strength caused the defeat of a Tory government. Labour won both elections of 1974 with a pledge to repeal the 1971 Industrial Relations Act and to restore free collective bargaining. Clearly the new government had learned its lessons from the failure of previous attempts to curb trade union strength via the former Labour government's *In Place of Strife* and the even greater ignominy of Edward Heath's 1971 Act. Despite the growing problem of unemployment, trade union membership continued to rise, as did the class combativeness of key sections of the trade union movement. The TUC was thus willing to enter into an agreement with the government commonly known as the 'Social Contract'. In return, the government fulfilled its promise of enacting a raft of progressive legislation. But, at the same time, the International Monetary Fund (IMF) forced the Labour government to introduce significant cuts in social expenditure as the price of being a debtor nation. It was also a period in which the Conservative Party changed its leadership to hard-line neoliberalism and began to plan a massive attack on the labour movement. Right-wing organisations and newspapers had already begun this – the Freedom Association bankrolled the Grunwick lockout in 1976, and managements in some key workplaces, especially the Midlands car industry, were victimising left-wing shop stewards. Such actions were supported and encouraged by an increasingly powerful news media exemplified by Rupert Murdoch's acquisition of *The Sun* and the *News of the World* in 1969.

In 1978, Moss Evans succeeded Jack Jones as Transport and General Workers' Union (TGWU) general secretary. Evans withdrew from the Social Contract and backed members who went on strike in order to retrieve their loss of real income since 1975. Many other strikes, especially among public sector workers, followed suit in 1979. This was met with an unprecedented and orchestrated press attack, dubbing the strike wave as the 'winter of discontent'. This opened the way to a Tory election victory in 1979 with Margaret Thatcher as prime minister. The Tories capitalised on the industrial unrest and, together with their supporters in the mass media, embellished the still widely accepted myth of over-mighty trade unionists holding the country to ransom. This was the justification for their long-held desire to introduce anti-union legislation, a promise they made in their 1979 manifesto.

The Tory onslaught which followed led initially to mass trade union opposition, in particular by the miners and the printers. However, the defeat of the year-long miners' strike (1984–1985) and of the Wapping dispute (1986–1987) strengthened the government's hand by showing that the best organised and most militant trade unions could be defeated. The state's determination to defeat organised labour led to a sustained attack on trade unions and an assault on working-class living standards and the welfare state. Unsurprisingly, trade union membership declined in the Thatcher years, leading to a bleak period of industrial defeat and union retrenchment, characterised by mergers and reorganisation.

Economic Background, 1974–1992

The 1970s as a whole witnessed periods of exceptionally high inflation, weak overall growth, volatile balances of payments, rising unemployment and shifts in income distribution from earners to owners.[2]

Part of the problem was credit easing, leading to a housing boom and inflationary wage–price spirals creating the conditions in which unionised workers were playing catch-up with prices. Incomes policies were designed to break this vicious circle, but did so, or at least intended to do so, by forcing pay restraint and reducing the standard of living for most workers. As usual, the burden fell on the most vulnerable parts of the labour force – part-time women workers, immigrants and non-unionised service sector workers.

As was shown in *Unite History*, volume 4, the previous Tory government bequeathed high rates of inflation fed by the growth of credit. The resulting inflation (25 per cent by 1975) was mainly as a result of these policies, although the 1973 oil crisis meant a 70 per cent jump in oil prices adding to workers' woes (Figure 1). One consequence was wage increases backed by strong union action and strikes.

By 1974, the recession was biting deep into working-class lives with a sudden fall in output (3.4 per cent) and the highest unemployment since the 1930s. This posed hard questions for the unions and the new Wilson government. The era of cheap oil and the British state's deliberate encouragement of road building and car and lorry use meant that when petrol prices doubled living standards fell.

Another dominant consequence of the Heath government's policies and the oil crisis was the persistent balance of payments deficit. With rising prices and rising imports, the political centre of debate shifted to trade and financing the current account deficit. The Labour government

2 I am grateful to Roger Seifert (author of *Unite History*, vol.2) for much of this information.

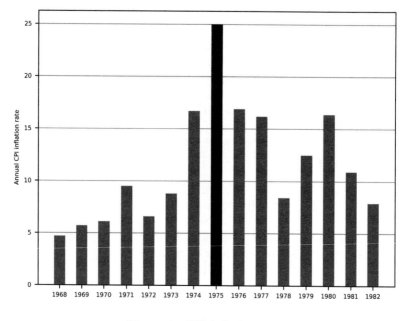

Figure 1: UK inflation 1970s
(Office for National Statistics)

sought peace with the unions and control over wages through the Social Contract and its attendant elements of favourable labour laws in exchange for incomes policy limits.

This culminated in the disastrous decision by Chancellor of the Exchequer Denis Healey to seek assistance from the IMF in the form of a bailout. This was partly in panic over the falling pound, and partly in an effort to avoid another bout of stagflation. Equally disastrous were the IMF demands – deep and lasting spending cuts which were implemented in 1976–1977. While they did help stabilise inflation and allowed some very modest growth in GDP, overall the impact on people's lives was terrible. It was as if the Labour government was launching a class war against its own supporters. The consequences for the government were dire, as the 1979 general election was to show.

In 1981, a deep recession hit, deliberately created by the new Thatcher government. It meant the collapse of the traditional manufacturing sector, with unemployment rising to 3 million. The economy and employment did not recover until the mid-1980s, with Thatcher's second term in office, which was characterised by another boom (Figure 2). While wages did recover, the real boom was again in housing and in stocks. As if the lessons of history were irrelevant, this boom came to a sudden and expected end with another mini-recession in 1991.

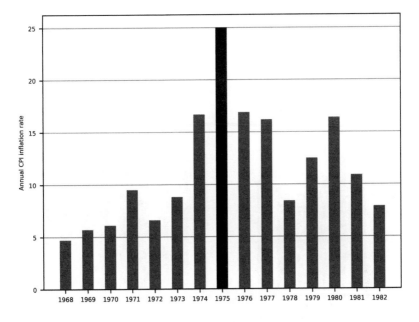

Figure 2: UK inflation 1980s
(Office for National Statistics)

Economic reforms focused on supply-side solutions with a rash of privatisations across the utilities (water, gas, electricity, telephones), airlines, a range of smaller highly profitable state enterprises and a rhetoric of free markets. But this was accompanied by legal restrictions on workers' rights and unions' abilities to protect their members. At the same time, industry was deregulated.

Alongside the usual raft of policies to control inflation through government cuts, higher taxes and lower wages came the money supply debate. Aggregate demand fell due to an overvalued pound, and recession again showed the deep nature of boom and bust – or the contradictions inherent in British capitalist economics. As always, the recession meant high unemployment was used to control wages better than any incomes policy. It was the manufacturing sectors in Scotland, Wales and the North of England that were hardest hit.

The Thatcherites believed that they had cracked the nut of sluggish growth in the early 1980s (reaching 8 per cent without inflation). But this was a mirage since Chancellor of the Exchequer Nigel Lawson's shadowing of the German currency created a false impression of sound money while in the real world prices were rising and the balance of payments was falling. This economic boom was followed by another recession. Interest rates were pushed up, consumer debt was too high

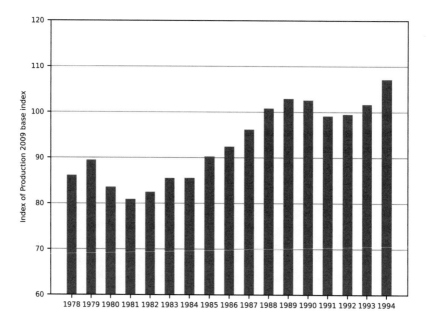

Figure 3: Index of UK industrial production
(Office for National Statistics)

and not sustainable, and confidence in the policies and the real economy
collapsed. One sign was the fall in house prices, sharpening the levels of
disharmony with the Tory party. More importantly, government policy
and the terms of trade meant a sharp decline in heavy industries of coal,
steel and shipbuilding. The recession in the late 1980s recreated the
current account deficit due to growth in imports, decline in the competitiveness of UK industry (despite the boasts of the Thatcherites that they
had made the economy more efficient) and the rise of London as the city
of finance (Figure 3). For many, the worst feature of these years was the
waste of the revenues from the North Sea oil reserves. A massive opportunity was lost to reinvigorate British economy and society rather than
simply line the pockets of the rich at the expense of the working class.

1

The TGWU and the Labour Government

The general election of February 1974 saw the return of a minority Labour government led by Harold Wilson. Clearly effective government was difficult in such circumstances. Nonetheless, within the nine months of its tenure, Labour fulfilled one of its most important manifesto pledges – it repealed the Industrial Relations Act and established the Advisory, Conciliation and Arbitration Service (ACAS). In October 1974, a second general election was held, and although Labour was returned again its majority of only three did not augur well, especially in view of what Wilson described as Britain's 'most dangerous crisis since the war'.[1] The nature of the crisis was spelt out in its February manifesto, which described a series of interlocking crises.

> Prices are rocketing. The Tories have brought the country to the edge of bankruptcy and breakdown. More and more people are losing their jobs. Firms are going out of business. Housing costs are out of reach for so many families. The Common Market now threatens us with still higher food prices and with a further loss of Britain's control of its own affairs.[2]

The new government, having learned its lessons from the failure of the previous Labour government's *In Place of Strife* and Heath's 1971 Industrial Relations Act, was not going to be allowed to forget them. The two biggest unions in Britain now had left-wing socialists as leaders – Jack Jones of the TGWU and Hugh Scanlon of the Amalgamated Union of Engineering Workers (AUEW). The two became known as

1 October 1974 Labour Party manifesto. http://labour-party.org.uk/manifestos/1974/Oct/1974-oct-labour-manifesto.shtml.

2 February 1974 Labour Party manifesto. http://labour-party.org.uk/manifestos/1974/Feb/1974-feb-labour-manifesto.shtml.

'the terrible twins'. The inescapable conclusion was that the trade union movement in the 1970s was still a force to be reckoned with, and although the Communist Party had an undoubted influence among the activists through such organisations as the Liaison Committee for the Defence of Trade Unions (LCDTU), it would be indulging in conspiratorial fantasy akin to Tory propaganda to write off this 'forward march' as the work of a few dangerous, politically motivated militants. Despite the growing problem of unemployment (which stood at half a million when Labour took office and had risen to one and a half million in 1979), trade union membership continued to rise, as did the class combativeness of key sections of the trade union movement.

The TUC leadership was easily satisfied with the accommodating attitude of the Labour government and readily accepted, on behalf of the trade unions, the joint agreement with the government commonly known as the Social Contract. It meant that the TUC would accept voluntary wage restraint in return for the abolition of the 1971 Act and the promise of affirmative rights for trade unions. This formed the basis of Labour's election manifesto of October 1974 from which the following extract is taken:

> At the heart of this manifesto and our programme to save the nation lies the Social Contract between the Labour Government and the trade unions, an idea derided by our enemies, but certain to become widely accepted by those who genuinely believe in government by consent – that is, in the democratic process itself as opposed to the authoritarian and bureaucratic system of wage control imposed by the Heath government and removed by Labour. The Social Contract is no mere paper agreement approved by politicians and trade unions. It is not concerned solely or even primarily with wages. It covers the whole range of national policies. It is the agreed basis upon which the Labour Party and the trade unions define their common purpose.[3]

The TGWU, having campaigned vigorously for the return of a Labour government, was an enthusiastic supporter of the Social Contract, which it regarded as essential in the light of the economic crisis (a crisis which, according to its General Executive Council (GEC), must 'necessarily limit the government's freedom to act').[4] It added that the real meaning of the Social Contract was that economic burdens had to be shared equitably, but emphasised strongly, despite fears to the contrary, that the government

---

3 October 1974 Labour Party manifesto.
4 Modern Records Centre (MRC), University of Warwick, MSS.126/TG/1186/A/52. Minutes of the General Executive Committee, 2 December 1974.

'had no intention of re-introducing a wage freeze or statutory control of incomes. The commitment to voluntary collective bargaining was an integral part of the Social Contract.'[5] As we shall see, this optimism proved to be misplaced.

The Rise and Fall of the Social Contract

Although the Social Contract was described by the activists and forces on the left of the movement as a 'con-trick' – an expedient to stem the tide of militancy and bind workers into an acceptance of 'the system' – it is easy to understand the seductive power of the Social Contract.[6] Unlike that offered by New Labour in the 1990s, this one offered much and delivered a series of genuine reforms, including in 1974 the Health and Safety at Work Act, the Trade Union and Labour Relations Act, the Equal Opportunities Commission and the Sex Discrimination Act 1975. In addition, as one historian of the period has arguably overstated, cabinet ministers in the 1974–1979 government were 'willing to defend union rights publicly, on a scale and with a regularity that has no recent parallel in British political history'.[7] While this was true of the first twelve months of the new government as it sought to undo the damage inflicted by the Tories, good relations with the trade union movement did not survive. The government, as promised, repealed the 1971 Industrial Relations Act and replaced it with the Trade Union and Labour Relations Act. This was amended in 1976 to broaden the protection for trade disputes and to remove some of the barriers the Tories had introduced in relation to the closed shop. Despite this, loopholes in the law remained as the Grunwick dispute of 1976–1978 clearly showed. The Employment Protection Act (EPA) of 1975 was a highly significant piece of legislation in that for the first time it gave statutory rights to shop stewards and union representatives and awarded them time off for trade union activity and training. The Health and Safety at Work Act 1974 (HSWA) did the same for newly introduced trade union Safety Representatives. These two acts ushered in a massive expansion of trade union education conducted by the TUC and affiliated unions, which, to a limited extent, survives to this day. The EPA also accorded statutory power to the new Advisory, Conciliation and Arbitration Service and established the Employment Appeals Tribunal. In addition, the Act established rights to maternity pay and a guaranteed right for women to return to their job after maternity leave.

5 Minutes of the General Executive Committee, 2 December 1974.

6 This contradictory superficial allure was expressed in the title of a Communist Party pamphlet: Bert Ramelson, *Social Contract: Cure-All or Con-Trick?* (Communist Party of Great Britain, 1974).

7 David Coates, *Labour in Power* (Longman, 1980), p.58.

Certainly this was a very promising beginning, but it foundered on the issue of government economic policy and specifically its incomes policy. The attempt to control incomes first by voluntary and later by statutory means ultimately proved a major barrier to the unions' jealously guarded right to free collective bargaining especially in the public sector, over which government policy had more control. Initially there was no statutory wage control. TUC leaders advocated voluntary wage restraint as a quid pro quo, in the spirit of the Social Contract, for the government's social reforms. However, this did not satisfy Labour's desire for counter-inflationary measures. Critics of the government were equally critical of the TUC for entering into such a historically unprecedented agreement 'to collaborate with the government and the employers to cut real wages, and to police the implementation of the cuts'.[8] Similarly, critics on the left argued that the Social Contract did not represent a genuine quid pro quo arrangement since in return for agreeing to a £6 maximum pay increase, the government had agreed only to acts of elementary justice, which were Labour Party conference policy anyway, pre-dating the Social Contract. It was clear by 1975 that the government favoured a statutory incomes policy predicated upon the orthodox Treasury mantra that high wages are the main cause of inflation. This thinking was emblazoned in very bold type on the back page of a widely distributed government pamphlet, which quoted Wilson as saying: 'One man's pay rise is not only another man's price rise: it might also cost him his own job – or his neighbour's job.'[9] Contemporary critics of the government[10] argued that almost from the outset the government went as far as to reject the traditional social democratic Keynesian model[11] as the price to be paid for European Economic Community (EEC) membership and loans from the International Monetary Fund and the Central Bank.[12] Tony Benn, a

8 Bert Ramelson, *Bury the Social Contract: The Case for an Alternative Policy* (Communist Party of Great Britain, 1977), p.2.

9 *Attack on Inflation: A Policy for Survival. A Guide to the Government's Programme* (HMSO, 1975), p.9. https://wdc.contentdm.oclc.org/digital/collection/tav/id/61/. This was a popular guide to the White Paper, *Attack on Inflation: A Policy for Survival* (HMSO, 1975).

10 See, for example, the collection of essays in Ken Coates (ed.), *What Went Wrong: Explaining the Fall of the Labour Government* (Spokesman, 1979).

11 A fact fully acknowledged by Denis Healey in his autobiography, *The Time of My Life* (Penguin, 1990), p.378.

12 This view, that the EEC referendum marked a decisive turning point in Labour government policy and practice, is also held by later writers. See, for example, Hugh Kerr, 'Labour's Social Policy 1974–79', *Critical Social Policy*, 1981, vol.1, no.1, pp.1, 5; David Coates, 'Labour Governments: Old Constraints and New Parameters', *New Left Review*, September–October 1996, vol.1, no.219. https://newleftreview.org/issues/i219/articles/david-coates-labour-governments-old-constraints-and-new-parameters.pdf.

minister in the Labour government, went further. He argued that such labour principles and policies were already 'Thatcherite' even before the election of the 1979 Tory government. Thatcherism, he wrote, 'had become the philosophy of the British establishment long before Margaret Thatcher became prime minister, and had paved the way for the intellectual dominance of right-wing ideas throughout the Eighties.'[13]

Stuart Holland opined that 'Labour since 1974 has managed British capitalism in a manner which would have been inconceivable for British Conservatism of either the Heath or Thatcher variety'.[14] While there was general acknowledgement that inflation was a very serious problem, there was growing opposition to the increasingly monetarist turn in Labour's economic policy as a method of dealing with the deepening economic crisis. The left advocated an Alternative Economic Strategy (AES) that gradually won widespread acceptance within many unions and constituency Labour parties. This strategy argued for a range of demands including import controls, reduced expenditure on armaments, withdrawal from the EEC, increased public expenditure, greater state investment in British industry, a shorter working week, the redistribution of wealth and a return to free collective bargaining.

While not accepting all elements of the AES, the TGWU accepted the left's view of the EEC (widely known then as the Common Market) and campaigned vigorously against continued membership in the 1975 referendum. Jack Jones had been a consistent opponent of Britain's application for membership and final entry in 1973. He had argued that an election or a referendum should decide the issue. The Labour Party agreed, and hence its 1974 election manifesto promised a referendum on the grounds that

The Common Market now threatens us with still higher food prices and with a further loss of Britain's control of its own affairs. We shall restore to the British people the right to decide the final issue of British membership of the Common Market. The British people were never consulted about the Market.[15]

Surprisingly, given this statement, the Labour leadership campaigned for a 'yes' vote. Knowing that opposition to the EEC was popular among the TGWU membership – particularly among lorry drivers who opposed the imposition of the tachograph ('the spy in the cab') – Jones was very active in the 'Get Britain Out' campaign. He shared many anti-market platforms

13 Tony Benn, *Conflicts of Interest: Diaries, 1977–80* (Arrow Books, 1991), p.xi.
14 Stuart Holland, 'Capital, Labour and the State', in Coates, *What Went Wrong*, p.207.
15 February 1974 Labour Party manifesto.

with Tony Benn, Michael Foot, Peter Shore and, controversially, on one occasion with Enoch Powell. The grounds of Jones's opposition to the EEC was stated clearly in his 21st quarterly report to the GEC:

> Fundamentally the Rome Treaty is based on [...] the 'laissez faire' philosophy of the last century which we in our movement do not accept. [...] a supra-national body in Brussels is definitely not appropriate to determine national policies. The reality of a nation is still of supreme importance.[16]

The TGWU, the Social Contract and Incomes Policy

As the largest trade union in Britain, the TGWU, with its secretary Jack Jones, was central to initiating, supporting and implementing the Social Contract. Jones himself, in his autobiography, acknowledges that he was one of the architects of the Social Contract, the origins of which were formulated in the Labour Party–TUC Liaison Committee, an organisation founded in 1972 on the initiative of Jones.[17] This body was intended to form a close unity between the leadership of the trade union movement and the Labour Party (Figure 4). Its significance was all the more important now that Labour was the party of government. Jones recounts that he vigorously supported the Social Contract throughout.[18] He saw it as the only antidote to mounting unemployment. His argument rested on the assumption that excessive wage increases would lead to the closure of the many firms which could not afford to pay the rises, thereby increasing unemployment. This line of thinking was attacked by the left, as evidenced at the TUC congress of 1974. A motion, proposed by Jones, to support the Social Contract was opposed by three left-wing union leaders, Ken Gill, Hugh Scanlon and Bill Ronksley.[19] These opponents were ultimately persuaded to withdraw their opposition, which, as Jones notes, drew the ire of the *Morning Star*. Together with the Communist Party, the paper argued that the Social Contract was merely a revamped version of the previous government's enforced phase 3 wage restraint. But although Jones was attacked for his support for wage curbs he was sure that if he 'did not make a stand, no-one would'.[20]

16 MRC MSS.126/TG/1186/A/52. Minutes of the General Executive Committee, 2 December 1974, Appendix II.
17 Jack Jones, *Union Man: The Autobiography of Jack Jones* (Collins, 1986).
18 Jones, *Union Man* for textual references.
19 Representing (in order) the following unions: Technical, Administrative and Supervisory Section (TASS), Amalgamated Union of Engineering Workers (AEUW), Associated Society of Locomotive Steam Enginemen and Firemen (ASLEF).
20 Jones, *Union Man*, p.288.

TUC - LABOUR PARTY LIAISON COMMITTEE

ECONOMIC POLICY AND THE COST OF LIVING

This has been drawn up by the
TUC – Labour Party Liaison Committee
and approved by the TUC General Council, the
National Executive Committee and the
Parliamentary Committee of the Labour Party

3p.

Figure 4:
TUC–Labour Party
Liaison Committee,
'Economic Policy and
the Cost of Living' –
1973 publication that
would form the basis
of the Social Contract
(TUC Library
Collections)

Even when, in 1976, with rising unemployment and rising inflation, the attack on the Social Contract was much more widespread in the trade union movement, Jones maintained his strong support for it. Echoing Wilson, his view was that inflation caused price rises and this had led to increased demands for higher wages. In this respect Jones adopted the disquieting analysis of the Labour government's White Paper on inflation, which reflected the traditional Treasury view.

A continuation of present rates of inflation would gravely damage the social and economic fabric of the nation and threaten us with external bankruptcy. To cure inflation by unemployment would cause widespread misery, industrial strife and the degeneration of our productive capacity. The only sensible course is to exercise pay restraint and to reduce our domestic inflation without sacrificing our long-term economic goals.[21]

21 Draft White Paper on Inflation, Note by the Secretary of the Cabinet, 8 July 1975 (typescript), p.2. The National Archives, CAB 129/184/1. http://filestore.national-archives.gov.uk/pdfs/small/cab-129-184-c-76.pdf.

As a compromise position, Jones's answer was to promote the claim for flat rate wage rises. The TGWU Biennial Delegate Conference (BDC) in 1975 voted for the flat rate policy. In the same year, Jones successfully persuaded the TUC to agree to a flat rate £6 pay rise for all those earning under £8,500 p.a., arguing that championing this policy was 'not a free for all, but a fair for all'.[22] Above all, Jones was determined to save the Labour government. He had been told by Wilson and Barbara Castle that some members of the cabinet had predicted a government defeat on the issue of wages and inflation and were preparing for a possible coalition. This information was well founded. In March 1977, the Conservatives were planning a 'no confidence' vote in the Labour government. If it passed, the government would be forced to resign and call a general election. To circumvent this Callaghan held meetings with Liberal MPs, from which emerged a Lib–Lab pact. Thirteen Liberal MPs pledged to support the Labour government 'in return for being consulted over a range of economic and social policies, as well as a parliamentary vote on the use of proportional representation for elections to the European Parliament'.[23]

However, this agreement was short-lived – the Liberals withdrew in the summer of 1978, so Callaghan had to seek support from the nationalist parties (Scottish and Welsh), both of which wanted to delay the election. Their support was contingent on the government's promise of support for Scottish and Welsh devolution. This, together with the expectation that the trade unions would support a fourth year of pay restraint, was sufficient for Callaghan's ill-fated decision to delay the calling of a general election until May 1979 instead of, as had been expected, autumn 1978.

His opposition to a possible Lib–Lab coalition and his continuing support for pay restraint help to explain Jones's avowal that, throughout its tenure, whatever his misgivings, he 'was determined to back the government warts and all'.[24] The flat rate pay figure had been agreed after awkward negotiations between Jones and Denis Healey. However, a year later, with runaway inflation and massive price rises, the battle for wage increases was unstoppable. In 1976, after Wilson's surprise resignation, Jim Callaghan took over as prime minister. The International Monetary Fund (IMF) demanded drastic cuts in public spending. Tony Benn argued for the well-formulated and widely accepted AES, but his proposals were rejected.

It has been argued that Callaghan and Healy's rejection of the left alternative to the economic crisis (the AES) represented something more than just a rejection of Keynesianism and a reversion to orthodox

22 Quoted in H.M. Drucker, 'The Influence of the Trade Unions on the Ethos of the Labour Party', in Ben Pimlott and Chris Cook (eds), *Trade Unions in British Politics: The First 250 Years* (Longman, 1991), p.193.

23 Peter Dorey, *'Should I Stay or Should I Go?': James Callaghan's Decision Not to Call an Autumn 1978 General Election* (Macmillan, 2016).

24 Jones, *Union Man*, p.299.

economics.[25] Mitchell argues that Denis Healey was, by 1976, convinced that 'Monetarism' was a valid alternative to Keynesianism and that an IMF loan was the only answer. In order to gain acceptance for the 'no alternative' (to the IMF) position, Healey and Callaghan worked hard

> to construct the situation as a crisis of massive proportions although much of the 'crisis' was the result of their extreme reluctance to allow the pound to depreciate, to impose capital controls to stop the non-productive speculative outflows that were causing the currency to drop in value [...] in doing so, the British government effectively created their own 'funding' crisis.[26]

Public sector unions were particularly affected by these public spending cuts. The National Union of Public Employees (NUPE), whose membership was 100 per cent public sector workers, fought back. NUPE was the leading force behind the newly formed National Steering Committee Against the Cuts (NSCAC), which organised a one-day strike in November 1976 against the cuts. In these circumstances it was clearly more difficult to retain support for the Social Contract. However, such was the desire to maintain a Labour government that Healey's proposal for a flat rate increase of 3 per cent was reluctantly accepted by the TUC and by the General Executive Council of the TGWU, but this effort was, as Jones put it, 'not sufficient to stem the tide of disgruntlement against the government',[27] and despite his efforts urging moderation in pay claims the TGWU BDC in July 1976, after a stormy debate, passed a motion calling for 'unfettered collective bargaining'. Jones described this as a 'momentous defeat'.[28]

It was also a defeat for the government's pay policy. Healey acknowledged that even with the support of trade union leaders it was difficult to operate a pay policy in Britain, because, in his view, 'the real power lies not in the union headquarters but with the local shop stewards, who tend to see a rational incomes policy as robbing them of their functions. Moreover, the TUC has no real power over its constituent unions.'[29]

Healey's view was apparently confirmed by the growth in strike activity in both private and public sectors in 1976–1977. By 1976, the government, with the agreement of the TUC, sought to impose a 4.5 per cent wage ceiling. However, given that prices were rising (as was unemployment), there was increasing opposition to wage control, and 1976–1977 witnessed

25 See Bill Mitchell, 'The British Left is Usurped and IMF Austerity Begins 1976' (blog), 29 June 2016. http://bilbo.economicoutlook.net/blog/?p=33907.
26 Mitchell, 'The British Left'.
27 Jones, *Union Man*, p.325.
28 Jones, *Union Man*, p.326.
29 Healey, *Time of My Life*, p.399.

a major growth in strike activity.[30] Clearly, the Social Contract was now a dead duck.

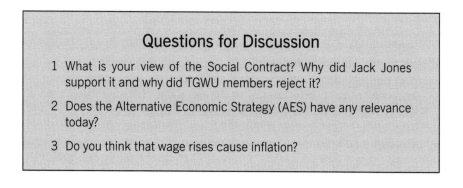

Questions for Discussion

1 What is your view of the Social Contract? Why did Jack Jones support it and why did TGWU members reject it?

2 Does the Alternative Economic Strategy (AES) have any relevance today?

3 Do you think that wage rises cause inflation?

---

30 Discussed in Chapter 3.

2

Industrial Militancy, 1974–1977

Trade Unions Fight On

The early years of the Labour government continued to witness trade union militancy. However, one of the most significant aspects of the fightback in this period was the involvement of trade union members previously largely ignored by the labour movement: black workers and women workers. Most unions in the 1970s had a poor record in recognising, let alone combating, sex and race discrimination in the workplace or among their own members. Despite the Race Relations Act 1976 and the 1975 Sex Discrimination Act – which made it unlawful to discriminate against a person directly or indirectly in the field of employment – racism and sexism, as deeply ingrained divisive ideologies, were endemic in society and in the labour movement.[1] Three strikes in this period were led by black workers and women workers and, as will be seen, had an important impact in changing trade union policies and internal practices.

Some of the strikes from 1974 to 1978 were official, many were not. Three official strikes and one unofficial strike were particularly important, attracting as they did widespread trade union support. The successful 1976 Trico equal pay strike, led by women, was officially supported by the AUEW. This was the first victorious equal pay strike for over 50 years. Similarly, the Grunwick strike of 1976–1978 was initially backed by the Association of Professional, Executive, Clerical and Computer Staff (APEX). It received massive trade union support including from the TGWU. The eight-week national firefighters strike for a 30 per cent wage increase and a reduction in working hours was an official Fire Brigades Union-backed strike which also attracted widespread support from trade unions. The TUC backed the Labour government's opposition to the firefighters' strike even when the government declared a state of emergency

---

1 A fuller examination of trade union responses to racism and sexism is covered in Chapter 8.

and used the armed forces to fight fires, using the military's fleet of 1950s 'Green Goddess' fire engines.

However, a widely supported strike involving TGWU members at Imperial Typewriter was unofficial. Despite the alleged pro-union policy of the government, it nonetheless displayed hostility to all industrial action, and the Home Secretary, Merlyn Rees, played a key role in both mobilising strong-arm tactics against the pickets and persuading APEX and the TUC to withdraw support from the Grunwick strikers[2] and the firefighters.

Imperial Typewriter

The first of these strikes was at Imperial Typewriter in 1974. The Leicester factory, owned by the American multinational Litton Industries, employed 1,600 workers, 1,100 of whom were South Asian – women in the majority. Litton owned another typewriter factory in Hull. In Leicester, endemic racist employment practices, bolstered by substantial National Front activity, ensured that black workers suffered both overt and covert discrimination. They were paid less than their white counterparts, especially in relation to bonus pay. There were numerous additional discriminatory practices, leading initially to 39 women walking out in protest, soon to be joined by many other black workers. Workers at Imperial Typewriter were members of the TGWU, but the union not only failed to support the strikers but colluded with the racist practices of the employer with whom the TGWU negotiator and full-time official, George Bromley, maintained a cosy relationship. Bromley, in addition to his union role, was a magistrate and a stalwart right-wing member of the Leicester Labour Party. Bromley opposed the strike, declaring:

> The workers have not followed the proper disputes procedure. They have no legitimate grievances and it's difficult to know what they want. I think there are racial tensions, but they are not between the whites and [blacks]. The tensions are between those Asians from the sub-continent and those from Africa. This is not an isolated incident, these things will continue for many years to come. But in a civilised society, the majority view will prevail. Some people must learn how things are done.[3]

Unsupported by their union, the strikers did not receive strike pay. In spite of this the majority of those workers who walked out from Imperial's

2 See Jack Dromey and Graham Taylor, *Grunwick: The Workers' Story*, 2nd edn. (Lawrence & Wishart, 2016), pp.207–208.

3 Quoted in Ron Ramdin, *The Making of the Black Working Class in Britain* (Verso, 1987), pp.271–280.

factory stayed out and managed to bring out a further 500 workers with them. This withdrawal of labour had the desired effect: within a few days production fell to 50 per cent of the norm and fell much further as the strike entered its fifth week. The strikers were supported financially by community and political organisations. Although the strike was ultimately unsuccessful, it was a key moment in galvanising Asian working-class resistance in the UK. Additionally, despite the shameful role of the TGWU, the Asian strikers remained staunch trade unionists. Ron Ramdin quotes one of the strikers as saying, 'We have a high regard for what the union can achieve once it is determined to flex its muscles and to take up the genuine grievances of the workers. But for this to happen the trade union officials must be responsive to the genuine grievances of the members.'[4]

Between 1972 and 1975, in the wake of the mass redundancies and the closure of many factories, trade unionists fought back, utilising the tactic of factory occupations and 'work-ins'. Inspired by the Upper Clyde Shipbuilders (UCS) work-in of 1972, over 260 factory occupations took place in this period – two of these were at the Imperial Typewriter factories in Leicester and Hull. The staunch trade unionism of the striking Imperial Typewriter workforce was evidenced once again when Litton Industries announced the closure of these factories. In common with many others, these occupations were relatively short-lived. The workers in Leicester unsuccessfully sought a buyer for the firm, and after five months the occupation ended in July 1975. However, the failure of the occupation was also due to the lack of unity of the workforce. The bitter legacy of the strike revealed racist divisions which meant, in the words of two historians of the occupation movement,

> the blame for closure was diverted from Litton Industries, the parent company. The Leicester plant's Asian workers, perhaps the most likely to resist, were undermined by the attitude of their white co-workers. The latter, and the local union, saw the Asian workers' action as precipitating the closure which they thought would be temporary in order to remove 'troublemakers'.[5]

However, the occupation of the other Imperial Typewriter factory owned by Litton Industries in Hull, often overlooked, was well supported by the TGWU, and posed additional problems for the company. Although it too was unsuccessful, it attracted much support, as recounted here by Val Burn, one of the TGWU shop stewards involved in the occupation.

---

4 Ramdin, *The Making of the Black Working Class in Britain*.
5 Alan Tuckman and Herman Knudsen, 'The Success and Failings of UK Work-Ins and Sit-Ins in the 1970s: Briant Colour Printing and Imperial Typewriters', *Historical Studies in Industrial Relations*, 2016, vol.37, pp.113–139.

The Occupation of Imperial Typewriter, Hull 1975

Val Burn

[The factory] manufactured and made the only British electric typewriter, which was used and known as the no.1 electric typewriter throughout the world.

As it was the no.1 in the world, in September 1973, Litton Industries, an American company, took it over on the grounds to ensure it stayed at no.1 – obviously for the profit too, and also with a handout from the government. When taking it over they held a mass meeting with us, the union reps, and the full workforce, laying out their plans of how they saw the way forward, and the need for increased production to maintain the no.1 world position. The workforce achieved the ongoing increased production, as they saw it as [job] security.

In February 1974, some six months after them taking over, and we had all left work for the day – I was at home and about 6 p.m. my phone started ringing with calls from the members stating they had hand-delivered letters posted through their doors telling them the factory had closed and not to go back into work any more. [They were told] that they had to go to a meeting the following week for any outstanding wages to be paid and for arrangements for them to go back in the factory to pick up their personal belongings.

We, the union reps, received our letters after all the workforce received theirs – about 2 a.m. onwards. As union reps, we told people when they rang that we would be going to the factory next morning at 6.30 a.m., our usual time, to see what was going on, and would welcome them being there with us. When we all arrived (about 300 of the workforce), the gates were locked and there was a police presence at the gates. In the security gatehouse there was five senior management – one of them being the American director who had taken the September meeting about being no.1 in the world. He stood there smirking at us all.

The police stated it was peaceful and no problems, so they made to leave, and as they left someone shouted, 'Are we going over?' The result was that 300 of us climbed over the gates and confronted the management. We asked the management to leave. We escorted them out through the gates and then locked the big main gates. At 9 a.m. we rang the union office to tell them we had taken over the factory, telling the union about the letters the workers had received and how the management had gone about it.

Someone had also rung the local press to say what had happened and day 1 of the sit-in began. With reporters and TV cameras arriving at the gates, the word got out about the sit-in. The company about 10 a.m. had the electricity etc. switched off.

During the morning, the Hull TGWU docks reps came to the gates on the first day to ask what had happened, also how could they help (they also supplied the sit-in with 300 fish and chips that day). It turned out there were a consignment of 5,000 plus typewriters on the Hull docks awaiting shipment, which the dockers embargoed in support of the workers' sit-in.

Again, this showed how Litton Industries had dealt with this whole issue. This had been their plan all the time. We as the workforce quickly got ourselves organised with shifts, the women working the day shifts and the men the night shift (this was to stop any gossip or inference that it was not run correctly). The workers cleaned up the factory, took stock of everything, kept all the parts and machinery in tip-top condition in preparation for a possible takeover. The union officially contacted the MPs and also experts to look at the business, and a business plan for the future growth of electronic typewriters (which was, as we now know it, the beginning of computers).

The full workforce went up to London by train to march to parliament to meet with MPs. Along with the union, officially we met with Tony Benn, a cabinet minister for employment, who had our business plan thoroughly scrutinised, and then supported the plan to go before the appropriate cross-section committee.

After a sit-in of 181 days, we were told that the committee had turned us down and that Litton Industries were going to sue the government. Hence we were ordered to leave as this also meant that the sit-in people could also be sued in the courts too, thus possibly losing all they had (possibly their homes).

In view of all the information, a meeting with all the sit-in people was held, and after a long meeting it was decided that we would all come out together with our heads held high as we had been fighting to save not only our jobs but also a future for the next generation.

If one looks at the technical world today, and for those of us who knew the business plan when it was presented to the ministers, we believe and know that Hull could have been part of the technical world as we now know it.

As agreed at the meeting, all members of the sit-in gathered together on the site and along with the official of the union we left the site of Imperial Typewriter united as one, with our heads held high. The support from all over the country from the trade union family was and had [been] enormous – the donations we received kept the sit-in in food, warmth, etc., plus we could pay people and help their families during the sit-in, as people's benefits had been stopped.

Despite being unsuccessful, <u>trade union solidarity is something that you cannot beat</u>.

Grunwick

The Grunwick Film Processing Laboratories strike of 1976–1978 was initially backed by APEX, the union which the workers joined once the strike started. This almost two-year-long heroic struggle led by Asian women workers attracted mass support from trade unionists at rank-and-file and leadership levels (especially from Post Office workers, printers and miners). It was the very success of the action and the mass solidarity it engendered which prompted the state to release the full force of its repressive apparatus, including the brutal Special Patrol Group (SPG), used at Grunwick for the first time in an industrial dispute.

As we have seen, such support for non-white workers was a very rare occurrence in British trade union history, given its persistent failure to back strikes by black workers. This was true of the Mansfield Hosiery strike in Loughborough in 1972 and the strike at Imperial Typewriter in Leicester in 1974.

Despite the alleged pro-union policy of the government, it maintained its hostility to all industrial action, and the Home Secretary, Merlyn Rees, played a key role to subvert the Grunwick strike by authorising the deployment of the SPG to violently attack the pickets and then cajole APEX and the TUC to withdraw official support from the Grunwick strikers.[6] APEX, under the leadership of its then general secretary, Roy Grantham, having originally supported the strike, changed its mind towards the end of 1977 and withdrew strike pay from the Grunwick workers. Likewise, the TUC, which had also initially backed the strike, withdrew its support in June 1978.

The Downing Street file, released by the National Archives in 2007, shows that the dispute over union recognition of Grunwick's mainly female Asian workforce caused far more concern in government circles than was previously thought. Prime Minister Callaghan authorised surveillance of Arthur Scargill and the NUM as the Grunwick dispute escalated. The scrutiny of Scargill was ordered after Callaghan was told by a Home Office official, Graham Angel, that 'sources' – presumably police Special Branch – believed Scargill intended to bring 5,000 miners to picket Grunwick. At the height of the dispute in mid-1977, when 10,000-strong mass pickets clashed with 3,700 police as they tried to close down the factory, a special ministerial group, chaired by Merlyn Rees, met daily to report to the prime minister. Callaghan was so concerned that Scargill would try to escalate the dispute using thousands of flying pickets that he even asked the cabinet secretary to draw up a note reminding him of the lessons of the so-called battle of Saltley Gates in Birmingham, when flying mass pickets won a decisive victory during the 1972 miners' strike and helped to bring down Edward Heath's Conservative government.

---

6 See Dromey and Taylor, *Grunwick*, pp.207–208.

In terms of the mass mobilisation of trade union solidarity shown to the Grunwick workers, their strike was a success (Figure 5). For the first time in British labour history, the struggle of non-white women (mainly) workers was officially recognised by their union and received overwhelming support in word and deed from many trade unions at national and local levels. This is evidenced by the action of postal workers in refusing to

Figure 5: 'Defend Workers' Right to Organise.
Support Grunwick Strikers'
(TUC Library Collections: The Union Makes Us Strong)

handle mail from Grunwick (a vital aspect of the work of a film-processing factory) and the mass picketing during the summer of 1977. However, the strike ultimately failed.

The Labour government sought to diffuse the dispute, in time-honoured fashion, by setting up a Court of Inquiry under the chairmanship of Lord Scarman. This ensured that 'the battle was moved off the streets, the mass picketing was brought under control and the "illegal" blacking of Grunwick's mail was ended'.[7] Both the TUC and APEX saw the Scarman inquiry and eventual report as a basis for ending the dispute although the strike committee, supported by Brent Trades Council, the South East Region TUC (SERTUC) and the TGWU Region 1, were more cautious, having anticipated the recalcitrant attitude of the employer. The Scarman inquiry recommended both union recognition and reinstatement of the workers. However, George Ward, the employer, backed by the right-wing National Association for Freedom (NAFF), rejected the recommendations. Despite the valiant attempts of Jack Jones (and Hugh Scanlon and Ken Gill) in support of the strikers, the TUC and APEX withdrew their support and the workers' strike committee reluctantly announced the end of the dispute in June 1978. The Conservative Party and other members of the right wing saw this as a major political and ideological victory, preparing the ground for Conservative success in the 1979 general election and their subsequent curbing of the unions' power in the 1980s.

It has been argued that Grunwick marked a turning point in British industrial relations in that it 'exposed, although few recognised it at the time, the redundancy of previous successful union tactics faced with an altogether more strategic opposition which changed the "rules" of industrial relations'.[8] Dorey supports this view, arguing that Grunwick, for the Conservative Party, served as an example of the iniquity of trade unions, which, in turn, led to their anti-union strategy that they had first formulated in the 'Stepping Stones' document (see Chapter 5).

A subsequent cause célèbre for the ideological right's increasing anger and antipathy towards unions (and the Labour government deemed to be in thrall to them, and 'in their pockets') was the 1976–78 Grunwick dispute, which seemed to crystallize much of what was most objectionable about contemporary trade-unionism in Britain.[9]

7 Dromey and Taylor, *Grunwick*.

8 Jane Holgate, *Arise: Power, Strategy and Trade Union Resurgence* (Pluto Press, 2021), p.91.

9 Peter Dorey, 'The "Stepping Stones" Programme: The Conservative Party's Struggle to Develop a Trade-Union Policy, 1975–79', *Historical Studies in Industrial Relations*, 2014, vol.35, pp.89–116.

The Grunwick Strike, August 1976–July 1978

Gary Fabian

(Region 1, Unite Luton, retired members' branch) (edited extracts)

At the time, I was employed by a coach-building company called H. J. Mulliner Park Ward, situated at the entrance of the estate. I was at the time a shop steward, prior to becoming a senior shop steward and Chair of the Joint Shop Stewards Committee (JSSC). [...]

We mainly produced a motor car called the Rolls Royce Corniche. Passers-by always stopped and looked to admire the obvious skills that went into the production of the car.

When Grunwicks opened in the Cobbold Road estate, the workers walked by our shop and often stopped to look. There were young men but they were mainly women of South Asian origin. As with all passers-by, we engaged them in conversation, and during those many chats they raised some of the issues that the employer imposed on them. They were paid by cheque, for example – the cheques were given to them one at a time during the Friday lunch break. At the time, there existed the 'Truck Act', which meant that an employer had to pay their employees by the coin of the realm. It also left little time for lunch. However, that was the least of their problems. The hours were long, holidays were few and far between, and the pay was extremely low. They described to us the way they were treated by the boss and the supervision, which by today's standards would be described as a bullying culture. In the many conversations we had with the workers we repeatedly said that their only hope was to join a trade union. Very little notice was taken until the fatal day when, en masse, they said enough was enough. They streamed out of the factory, stopped and told us of their actions. The advice from me and others was to go straight away to the Brent Trade Council in nearby Willesden High Street and join the appropriate union. Later, I learned that is what they did. A bitter battle had begun. [...]

When we, as a trade union body, were brought up to speed with how things were and the intention of the Grunwick workers to fight for reinstatement – but with fair pay – and their determination to picket both plants, the works committee put their plight on the agenda and [resolved] to keep abreast of their activities, and it was also decided at that stage to give both financial and moral support to their dispute. The TGWU Convenor, Brian Eagles, took a personal interest and was a major factor in driving support onwards. [...]

Although the strike had the official backing of their union, APEX, very little activity happened from the trade union side for a period of time. On the other hand, the opposition had been extremely busy. For instance, they persuaded the local police that the estate where the smaller plant was should not be entered by the pickets and they should only be allowed to stand at the entrance to the estate, which meant that, frankly, this had little meaning, since workers and deliveries to all the other companies continued. [...]

The view that we took, as a works committee, and mirrored by the Trades Council, was that assistance with picketing was required. For our part, we looked at the most vulnerable times and felt that early in the morning would be extremely helpful, and volunteers from our ranks could do an hour's stint before starting work. In tandem with our decision, volunteers from the Trades Council opted for assisting daily in the morning and afternoon. [...]

The pressure from the workers' side mounted as the campaign grew. Trades councils began to get the message out to trade unions in workplaces, and daily visits to the picket lines grew in numbers. Workplace committees began to collect money to aid the dispute and sent stewards and other workers to assist in picketing, particularly at times when the scabs went in to work and came out, making things far more difficult for them. In response, the employer concentrated all the film production in just one plant, the one by Dollis Hill underground station. In addition, George Ward purchased an old bus to bring the scabs to work. So the picture became clear – no compromise by the employer whatsoever. The road he took with his supporters was to crush all resistance. [...]

As the strike went into the following year, the trade union movement further mobilised, giving more financial support – and made more visits to the Grunwick plant. For our part, we emptied all our central funds, not once, but on a number of occasions. We also increased our visit to the daily picket.

It was on one of those daily pickets, in the company of TGWU stewards and a friend of mine, Terry Ennis, that we witnessed the new tactics of the police. When the police were aware that the scabs' bus was close to the factory they began to line the road in order to stop the demonstrators, or, more importantly, the official pickets, from approaching the bus – and it happened on a daily basis. Very soon after this I noticed a considerable number of people – men and women – coming towards the protesters and moving in behind us. Good, I thought, more demonstrators. More chance to stop the bus. To my surprise, as the bus turned the corner and we naturally moved forward, the new arrivals pushed or attempted to push us into the road, and a number of those protesters were promptly arrested.

Rather than walking away, trade union pressure increased. More and more trade unionists and members of the public visited the picket line. The Students Union began to be involved, to great effect. The Post Office union increased its involvement and postmen and women that delivered films to be processed refused to deliver to Grunwicks.

At our next works committee meeting we decided to 'up' our commitment – not financially, as we had given everything we could and were still making donations. Our decision was to up our picketing. We would send our members out to stand on the picket line on a daily basis for a period of time. I was given the responsibility to organise the picketing. As picket master, I picked two or three people from different departments to do two-hour stints. I organised it on the basis of there never being less than eight at any one time. Volunteers who were mainly shop stewards would be paid from our funds. I recall a discussion with a senior manager. He broached the subject of deliberately causing the loss of production of Rolls Royce cars that we produced. He was right, of course, but the problems for the sacked Grunwick workers were far more drastic than the loss of a car or two – and I told him so. He walked away threatening me with all kinds of reprisals.

However, this new initiative did little to alter the outcome. The government's only contribution at the time was to ask the Grunwick owner to go to arbitration as a way of bringing an end to what was a long-running dispute. George Ward refused, as we expected, and his next move was to take the Post Office workers' union to court in order to reintroduce daily deliveries. [...]

With that battle won, he started printing articles in some of the major newspapers declaring that all the strikers were sacked, that he had a new group of dedicated workers he would employ on a long-term basis and that daily demonstrations would have little effect on his decisions.

Once again, the sacked Grunwick workers, Brent Trade Council and the many supporting unions began thinking about a new strategy. The idea was to move to mass picketing. The thinking was that a mass picket would be necessary to stop the daily bus from delivering the scabs to the factory. Although not possible to do each and every day, the morale of all concerned would be boosted by an attempt to achieve that – even if it was just one day. The message went out through the trade union movement to Trades Councils and union branches.

As the day drew nearer, our Joint Shop Stewards Committee agreed that we would send at least 20 stewards and activists to join the mass picket and protest. The pickets were led by Brian Eagles, the TGWU convenor. The 20 were made up of TGWU, NUSWCH&DE, AEU stewards and activists. Our plan was to meet at the end of Denzil Road, within view of Dudden Hill Road, which is where the bus carrying the scabs would come from. I parked my car at the bottom end of Denzil Road and walked up the length of the road towards where I thought the demonstration would begin. I quickly noticed a parked police coach. This was followed by at least 30 (or maybe more) coaches. Most were full of policemen, but two were empty as the police from these two were already in Dudden Hill Lane. Within minutes, people began to arrive, first in tens and twenties then in hundreds. This was followed by masses of young students, but more importantly miners. The NUM had turned out in large numbers, even bringing their brass band with them. There were also a team of solicitors and lawyers giving advice. We were told to shout out our name if arrested. They also handed out the phone number of the Brent Law Centre and explained exactly what people needed to do if they were arrested and taken away by the police.

The bus stop at the bottom of Dudden Hill Lane had a cover over it, obviously to keep the rain off passengers. A miner (NUM member) climbed to the flat top and with a loudhailer he began to direct pickets and protesters to different points in the lane and direct others to the Grunwick factory.

Our group, including my friend Terry Ennis, a TGWU steward, were directed to the top of the hill in Dudden Hill Lane, where the scabs' bus would come from. We walked to our designated area and when arriving we linked arms and stretched across the road. Nothing happened for a short period of time and we just stood and waited for the bus to arrive. We were shocked to see, not the bus, but police on horses approaching us, not five or ten, but it seemed to me that it was all the police horses they had, there were so many. As they got closer and closer we moved as tightly together as we could and the horses kept coming. Most of us put our heads down and just looked at the floor. Suddenly, I could feel the breath from the horses on the top of my head and down my neck. I clearly remember thinking, 'I could get killed here'. Time elapsed and just as suddenly there was an order shouted out and the horses began to go backwards and turn round and retreat. I was absolutely amazed, as were the people around me. I looked behind me and it became clear. There were hundreds and hundreds of people packed tightly, stretching right down the hill to the bottom. No way through for the horses or the bus. The thousands of demonstrators stood their ground all day. There were attempts by the police to move people away from the entrance of Grunwick by pushing and shoving them. Some demonstrators were directed to the factory entrance to bolster numbers. The police arrested a large number of people but couldn't handle that many protestors. As the day moved on it became clear that the bus would not arrive, so plan B was brought into play: a march through Willesden to Roundwood Park for a rally. The march was led by the NUM brass band at the front, with Arthur Scargill, President of the NUM, and Frank Cave, Vice President. The day was a massive success. The object was achieved. Unfortunately, the following day, with far less pickets and demonstrators, the scabs' bus did get in. There were a number of other mass pickets that were successful but not to the extent of the first one.

As for us at Mulliner Park Ward, shortly after this time we went into dispute ourselves as our annual wage negotiations proved to be fruitless. We, as craftsmen and women, had been campaigning for what we felt was parity with other workers with similar skills. We were producing cars, Rolls Royces and Bentleys, for royalty and millionaires and felt we deserved more.

On our shopping list was a rise of £30 a week, full holiday pay and full sick pay, as the latter had evaded us for years, and our view was enough was enough. Our strike began in September 1977 and ended on the 1st of January 1978. Our membership remained solid all the way through that dispute.

Never a need for any assistance with picketing, our workforce of TGWU, NUSWCH&DE, AEU and EETPU never faltered in 17 weeks.

During that time our strike headquarters were at Brent Trades Council. We occupied the next room to the Grunwick pickets and relations were extremely good – so good that at one of the mass pickets we were offered a bucket collection. Those were normally restricted to Grunwicks only. That bucket collection brought in a considerable amount of money for our ongoing dispute. We still attended their mass pickets and rallies but none attracted more people than the one I detailed earlier. Their strike continued into the following year and grew more difficult by the month. [...]

Our contribution to that was just not simply cash. We organised support. We invited Jack Dromey to attend and address a mass meeting at RR Mulliner Park Wards on the morning that the marches reached our area. As Chair of the Joint Shop Stewards Committee, I chaired the mass meeting. Alex Steel, the TGWU convenor, moved the motion that we as the workforce stop work at noon and join the marches and greet them at Wembley Town Hall. To enable enough of our joint membership to attend we hired six coaches, which we filled with our members.

The Grunwick strike will live on in the hearts and minds of all those involved, and we will remember it with pride. In my view, the Grunwick strike was the beginning of the 'winter of discontent' of 1978–1979. There were massive strikes in engineering and manufacturing. There was the bakers' strike, the grave diggers' strike and refuse workers, and of course the firefighters' strike that rolled on week after week, with the government bringing into play what was called 'Green Goddesses', driven by army personnel, used as an attempt to defeat the FBU, the firefighters' union. Sadly, all these events took place under a Labour government.

Questions for Discussion

1 What can unions learn from the Imperial Typewriter strike and the Grunwick dispute?

2 Why did the TUC withdraw backing for the Grunwick strikers?

3 Why was the Labour Party so hostile to the Grunwick strike?

3

The End of the Labour Government, 1978–1979

Given the scale of the opposition on the ground to pay restraint and the level of industrial militancy on other issues, the TUC no longer felt able to enter into a third round of pay policy. This, as Denis Healey acknowledged, created great problems for the government, which in hindsight he felt was handled badly and led to the defeat of Labour in the 1979 election. In 1978, the government unilaterally introduced a pay norm of 5 per cent. Of this Healey wrote:

> It was typical of the hubris which can overcome a successful government towards the end of its term. If we had agreed on a formula such as 'single figures' we would probably have achieved an earnings increase much smaller than we got; and we would certainly have been able to avoid the 'winter of discontent'.[1]

The 'Winter of Discontent'

Clearly, as events were to show, the TUC did not exert power over its affiliates. While Healey lamented these, for him, uncomfortable truths, it is, nonetheless, testimony to the continuing influence of the shop stewards movement that it was able to mount a challenge to the orthodoxy which sought to blame workers for the ills of capitalism. It is in this context that the strike wave of 1978–1979, pejoratively dubbed the 'winter of discontent' by Larry Lamb, editor of *The Sun*, must be seen. Acquired by Rupert Murdoch in 1969, this mass-circulation tabloid newspaper had shifted allegiance from Labour to the Tories and was a significant asset to the Thatcherite anti-union crusade.

Although the strikes of 1979 have been seen in the main as involving public sector unions, the challenge to the government's pay policy

---

1 Denis Healey, *The Time of My Life* (Penguin, 1990), p.398.

originated in the private sector and involved the TGWU in particular. Jack Jones, who had fought so hard to support the Labour government's desire to implement wage restraint, was succeeded as general secretary by Moss Evans, who now presided over the disintegration of the government's pay policy. In a report to the GEC, Evans, in rejecting press reports of a rift between the TGWU and the Labour Party, nonetheless stated his support for the Social Contract, but his unequivocal opposition to wage restraint: 'I have always regarded the Social Contract as marking the special relationship between the two wings of the Labour Movement and not as a pay policy agreement.'[2] Hence the accuracy of Tony Benn's view that the lesson of Jack Jones's defeat at the TGWU BDC in July 1976 was 'burned into [the] soul' of his successor.[3] By this time, union members had embarked on an unstoppable course of free collective bargaining.

The first salvo in the battle for collective bargaining versus the government pay norm came from workers at Ford. Ron Todd of the TGWU was the chair of the union-side negotiating committee at Ford. He was aware of rank-and-file opposition to Labour's incomes policy, and thus when, in September 1978, Ford management offered 5 per cent, it was met, starting in the Halewood plant in Liverpool, with an immediate walkout of around 10,000 workers in all Ford plants. The AUEW and the TGWU lost no time in declaring the strike official and presented management with the unions' claim for a £20 per week increase and a 35-hour working week. This was encapsulated in the slogan '£20 on the pay, 1 hour off the day'. One of the reasons for the success of the Ford strike was the change in the structure of collective bargaining, which, since 1969, had gradually been removed from full-time trade union officials to joint shop stewards committees at plant level. This was a strategy which was advocated by Jack Jones and was successfully operational at Ford. In 1978, Bernie Passingham, a TGWU convenor at the Dagenham plant, described the Ford National Joint Negotiating Committee (FNJNC) thus:

> At this point in time the convenors' committee has never been better organised in its history. We have a set-up which is recognised by the officials, correspondence is sent out to the chairman of the convenors and circulated then to all other convenors, i.e. all information goes directly back to the plants. Also, if we oppose anything in relation to the FNJNC they won't arbitrarily push it through. This has to have the consent of the convenors, and by that I mean the convenors, then works committee, right back to the stewards. The company know clearly that they're not going to

2 MRC MSS.126/TG/384/A/1. General Secretary, Quarterly Report to the General Executive Committee, December 1978.

3 Tony Benn, *Conflicts of Interest: Diaries, 1977–80* (Arrow Books, 1991), p.435.

go back to pre-1969, where you had a bunch of national officials agreeing to something: if we don't agree to it, they're in a right mix.[4]

The *Daily Mail* described the strike as an 'all-out war against Jim's 5 per cent'. The solid strike resulted in the unions' acceptance of a 17 per cent pay rise – a settlement which Callaghan later described as 'the heaviest blow, which did much to determine the course of events in the winter of 1978'.[5]

This was followed by another TGWU-backed strike, that of road haulage workers, in 1979. After a viciously hostile media campaign and the government's threat to call yet another state of emergency, a series of area settlements was negotiated, resulting in wage rises well above the 5 per cent norm and for reductions in working hours. Roy Mason, Secretary of State for Northern Ireland, said that the road haulage strike was the work of Communists and Trotskyists! It is clear that this strike and the failure of the government incomes policy rekindled Labour's unfulfilled preference for anti-union legislation. As we have seen, the Wilson government had attempted this in its 1969 *In Place of Strife* proposal but was forced to abandon the plan. However, the Callaghan government resurrected the aspiration to curb trade union militancy. Pre-empting the later Tory assault, Labour's suggestions, discussed in cabinet, bore a striking resemblance to the Thatcher government's anti-union laws. At a cabinet meeting in January 1979, dubbed by Tony Benn 'a cabinet to remember',[6] plans were discussed to outlaw secondary action, to issue a code of conduct to limit picketing and to withdraw state benefits for strikers. In addition, Callaghan argued for the removal of the right to strike for essential workers. Although these plans were not implemented during the lifetime of the government, they nonetheless prefigured the subsequent Tory anti-union laws of the 1980s.

Inspired by the road haulage strike and the successful nine-week Ford dispute, other workers took industrial action to redress the fall in real wages over the past five years. Public sector trade unions had seen a massive increase in their membership during the 1970s. Public sector workers in the NHS and local authorities were arguably the hardest hit by the cuts and they joined the action in great numbers. Women workers constituted a high percentage of the membership of public sector unions and their willingness to take action was particularly significant in the NHS, the care

4 Bernie Passingham, 'The Role of Shop Stewards'. Interview with Danny Connor and Bernie Passingham, *Marxism Today*, April 1978.

5 Quoted in Tara Martin López, *The Winter of Discontent* (Liverpool University Press, 2014), p.83.

6 Benn, *Conflicts of Interest*, pp.433–436.

sector and local education authorities.[7] A mass strike of 1.5 million public sector workers was held in January 1979 after the failure of negotiations on the joint union claim for a 35-hour week and a £60 minimum weekly wage for manual workers. The four major unions organising in the public sector (National Union of Public Employees (NUPE), Confederation of Health Service Employees (COHSE), General and Municipal Workers Union (GMWU) and the TGWU) rejected the government-imposed 5 per cent pay norm. Mass demonstrations were held in London, Cardiff, Edinburgh and Belfast in support of the unions' claim and in opposition to government policy, ushering in a programme of selective strike action. By March 1979, the number of working days lost (in this case due to strike action) was greater than during the Heath-imposed three-day week.

Aided by a supportive press, the Tories capitalised on the industrial unrest, and, together with their supporters in the mass media, contributed to the still widely accepted myth of over-mighty trade unionists holding the country to ransom. This was the justification for their long-held desire to introduce anti-union legislation, a promise they made in their 1979 manifesto. The Tories proposed three immediate changes. The first was to limit the right to picket to the worker's own place of work, thus making solidarity (or 'secondary') action illegal. Second, they promised to deal a blow to the 'objectionable weapon' of the closed shop by banning it altogether in the civil service and ensuring that elsewhere it could be sustained only if an overwhelming majority of the workers involved vote for it by secret ballot. Third, under the innocuous heading of 'Wider Participation', the Tories promised to introduce and fund secret postal ballots for union elections and other issues in order to counteract their assertion that 'Too often trade unions are dominated by a handful of extremists who do not reflect the common-sense views of most union members.'[8]

Callaghan's decision to delay the calling of a general election until spring 1979 – after the so-called 'winter of discontent' – is widely regarded as a disastrous mistake. This is based on the presumption that Labour could have won if the election had been held, as expected, in the autumn of 1978. An alternative view from the left suggested otherwise. Predicting the possible outcome of a general election *before* the strike wave of 1978–1979, Bert Ramelson (Communist Party industrial organiser) argued in 1977: 'The real question [...] is whether a Labour Government will be held responsible by the electorate for bringing about mass unemployment, drastic cuts in living standards [...] as well as drastically reduced social

---

7 See Lopez, *The Winter of Discontent*, for a full coverage of the hitherto neglected role of women workers in the public sector strikes of the 1970s.

8 1979 Conservative Party General Election manifesto. www.conservativemanifesto.com/1979/1979-conservative-manifesto.shtml.

services [and that this has] increased the chances of the return of a Tory government.'[9] In other words, Labour had abandoned its manifesto commitments well before 1979 and the IMF loan exacerbated the already existing politics of austerity. This, together with the imposition of meagre pay norms in a period of escalating inflation and massive IMF-dictated public sector cuts, accounts for the sharp decline in Labour's popularity.

Campaigning under the slogan 'Labour Isn't Working', the 1979 general election resulted in a massive victory for the Tories. The Conservatives won 339 seats compared with Labour's 269. The swing to the Conservatives of 5.2 per cent was the largest since 1945. However, blaming union militancy for the Tory victory buys in to the Thatcherite mantra of over-mighty unions holding the country to ransom. It thus exonerates the Healey/Callaghan leadership's espousal of neoliberal monetarist policies, the negative effects of which damaged working-class wages and living standards. It was this that caused Labour's election defeat.

9 Bert Ramelson, *Bury the Social Contract: The Case for an Alternative Policy* (Communist Party of Great Britain, 1977), pp.17–18.

4

Tory Strategy
and the Attack on Trade Unions

The Political Context: Thatcherism, Unemployment and the Attack on Trade Unions

The election of a Tory government in May 1979 was the first of four general election victories marking 18 years of uninterrupted Tory rule. It inaugurated a transformation of British politics sometimes known as 'Thatcherism'.[1] This policy was carefully crafted while the Tories were in opposition. Two private and confidential documents written in 1977 reveal this. One was the 'Ridley Report', dealing with the future of the nationalised industries, entitled 'Final Report of the Nationalised Industry Policy Group'.[2] It argued that 'denationalisation should not be attempted by a frontal attack, but by a policy of preparation [...] for return to the private sector by stealth',[3] and outlined a careful strategy for implementation.

> The Ridley Report was a detailed blueprint on how to firstly provoke, and secondly win, a battle against the so-called 'barriers' to monetarism. The report suggested several steps in order to achieve the stated, monetarist goals of 'fragmentation' and 'denationalization' of key industries. [...] [It] suggested that the first step on the road to privatization should be to provoke and attack one of Britain's powerful trade unions. The coal industry was suggested as the prime target.[4]

1 A term probably first used by Stuart Hall in the journal *Marxism Today* in January 1979.

2 Economic Reconstruction Group, 'Final Report of the Economic Reconstruction Group' ('Ridley Report'), Margaret Thatcher Foundation, Personal and Party Papers, Thatcher MSS (2/6/1/37). www.margaretthatcher.org/document/110795. The report was leaked to *The Economist* in May 1978 and attracted considerable controversy (particularly the 'Confidential Annex').

3 Ridley Report, p.22.

4 Phil Rawsthorne, 'Implementing the Ridley Report: The Role of Thatcher's Policy

The annex to the Ridley Report fired the first warning shot to the trade union movement. Written by Ridley himself, and entitled 'Countering the Political Threat', it envisaged union opposition to denationalisation, for he was convinced that 'There is no doubt that at some time the enemies of the next Tory Government will try and destroy this policy.'[5] This threat would, Ridley thought, 'emanate from a "vulnerable" industry, most likely coal, docks, or electricity'.[6] As we shall see, the report's recommendation that the coal industry should be the chosen target was acted upon eight years later. The Ridley Report was operationalised by its fervent adherents in Thatcher's Policy Unit throughout her tenure of office.

The second (and arguably the most revelatory) document was the 'Stepping Stones' Report, which outlined in some detail the new Tory ideology and the 'turn-around strategy' for its implementation.[7] Prefiguring the 1979 general election and the negative attitude to trade unions, the report argued that:

A landslide is needed, but it must represent an explicit rejection of socialism and the Labour–trades unions' axis; and the demand for something morally and economically better. The Tory Party's pre-election strategy must ensure that the preparation of policy includes plans for the removal of political obstacles to its implementation. There is one major obstacle – the negative role of the trades unions. [...] The principal objective is to persuade the electorate to reject Socialism, and also to reject its continued promotion by the trade union leadership, regardless of how the people have voted.[8]

For this to be achieved, a new type of Conservatism would be needed:

Britain's future is not going to be different from its past unless there are changes in attitudes and behaviour. But those changes are not going to stem from the policies of a party in government, if that party and its own attitudes have not changed. As long as the Tory Party is simply seen as the same institution making different noises, nothing will happen. [...] The task of the next Tory

Unit during the Miners' Strike of 1984–1985', *International Labor and Working-Class History*, 2018, vol.94, p.161.

5 Ridley Report, p.24.

6 Peter Dorey, '"It Was Just Like Arming to Face the Threat of Hitler in the Late 1930s": The Ridley Report and the Conservative Party's Preparations for the 1984–85 Miners' Strike', *Historical Studies in Industrial Relations*, 2013, vol.34, p.182.

7 'Stepping Stones' Report (1977), p.2. Margaret Thatcher Foundation, Personal and Party Papers, Thatcher MSS THCR (2/6/1/248). www.margaretthatcher.org/document/111771.

8 'Stepping Stones' Report, pp.S-1, S-2.

Government – national recovery – will be of a different order from that facing any other post-war government. Recovery requires a sea-change in Britain's political economy.[9]

This report, authored by two of Thatcher's policy advisors, Norman Strauss and John Hoskyns,[10] was followed in 1981 by a second (the Westwell Report). Taken together, they formed a detailed blueprint for the new 'Thatcherite' strategy and a 'Stepping Stones' guide for its implementation.

Founded upon the monetarist economic policies of Milton Friedman and Friedrich Hayek, Thatcherism rejected traditional Conservative strategy. Rather, it encompassed a programmatic reversal of post-war gains in health, welfare and social services. In the post-war period of 'consensus politics', Conservatives had, albeit reluctantly, supported the welfare state. Thatcherite conservatism reversed this policy and broke any semblance of consensus. Such reverses were to have dire consequences for the British labour movement. The government's monetarist policies were character-ised by a belief in free markets and a reduction of state intervention in the economy. This included the privatisation of state-owned assets, the deregu-lation of the market and of the financial industry, reductions in income tax and an openly hostile policy to trade unions. This last policy was central to Tory strategy since it regarded trade unions and collective bargaining as the biggest obstacle to capitalist regeneration and the free market.

Closures, Unemployment and the Fightback

Mass redundancies and closures in manufacturing industries help to account for the massively high rates of unemployment in the 1980s. Euphemistically termed 'restructuring', what Britain experienced was the steady decline of its industrial base. The early years of the Thatcher government witnessed the deepest economic recession since the 1929–1933 slump. Unemployment rose from 1.3 million in late 1979 to 3 million in April 1982. Despite the fact that the government manipulated the figures, unemployment remained at this level for several years. The second secret 'Stepping Stones' Report (the Westwell Report) candidly admitted this statistical manipulation: '[W]e should redefine unemployment so that only those actively seeking work should be classified as unemployed.'[11]

Although Britain's industrial decline pre-dated Thatcher, it was greatly accelerated during her tenure as prime minister (Figure 6). Since the

9 'Stepping Stones' Report, pp.37, S-1.

10 Hoskyns was head of the Downing Street policy unit from 1979 to 1982.

11 Westwell Report ('Stepping Stones to 1989') (draft of report), p.23. Margaret Thatcher Foundation, Churchill Archive Centre: Walters MSS (WTRS 1-14 f2). www.margaretthatcher.org/document/141997.

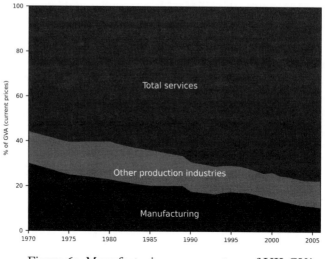

Figure 6: Manufacturing as percentage of UK GVA
(Office for National Statistics)

1980s, Britain saw the heaviest job losses in all major manufacturing industries located in the central belt of Scotland, the north of England (east and west), the Midlands and south Wales. Deindustrialisation and accompanying unemployment was not compensated by job growth in new industries or services, other than financial services. According to one pro-business commentator, the deregulation of financial services in 1986 – the 'big bang' – privileged City interests at the expense of manufacturing:

> One of the very controversial events was the 'big bang' of 1983 and the reorganisation of the City of London. You could argue that it was the big bang that cleared the way for 30 years of economic success for the UK financial sector. The British government stepped in and shook up the financial sector in a way that they failed to do for manufacturing, which was instead left to market forces to sort out.[12]

The People's March for Jobs

Echoing the unemployment marches of the 1930s organised by the National Unemployed Workers Movement, a significant protest movement

---

12 Graham K. Wilson, quoted in Ruth Strachan, 'Who Killed British Manufacturing?' *Investment Monitor*, 24 November 2020. www.investmentmonitor.ai/manufacturing/who-killed-british-manufacturing.

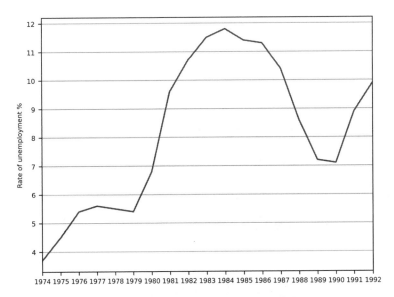

Figure 7: UK unemployment, 1980s
(Office for National Statistics)

against the mass unemployment of the 1980s was evidenced in the popular support for the two People's March for Jobs held in May 1981 and April 1983. Although the 1983 march was not initially supported by the TUC and the Labour Party, the TGWU, as in 1981, was an influential and powerful advocate for both marches. Ron Todd chaired the organising committee for the 1983 march, which started from Glasgow and culminated in a mass rally in Hyde Park, central London. The 1981 march started in Liverpool, largely on the initiative of the influential Merseyside 6/612 branch of the TGWU.[13] This branch was composed initially of car workers forced into redundancy by the closure of the Standard-Triumph plant in Speke in 1978. However, the branch had expanded to include many other unemployed workers following a wave of industrial closures on Merseyside (Figure 7).

These mass demonstrations of unemployed workers in the two marches for jobs clearly worried the government, especially since the final rally of 1983 People's March took place in June, four days before the general election. However, unemployment was an inevitable and incurable consequence of the Tories' monetarist strategy (Figure 8). In a Commons

---

13 For detailed information on TGWU 6/612 Branch, see Brian Marren, *We Shall Not Be Moved: How Liverpool's Working Class Fought Redundancies, Closures and Cuts in the Age of Thatcher* (Manchester University Press, 2016).

Figure 8: People's March for Jobs, April–June 1983
(TUC Library Collections)

debate on unemployment and the 1981 People's March for Jobs, the
Under-Secretary of State for Employment, Peter Morrison, said

> The efforts of the union representatives who organised the march
> would be better spent in trying to reach serious agreements
> with employers to make industry more competitive, which would
> be to the advantage of every worker in industry. That is a less
> glamorous, more difficult and demanding approach, but it is far
> more constructive.[14]

14 Hansard, HC vol.5, cols 589–595 (22 May 1981). https://api.parliament.uk/historic-
hansard/commons/1981/may/22/peoples-march-for-jobs.

In 1983, the Tories acknowledged in a confidential paper that the London rally might be a 'gift to the Labour Party', which, the paper (correctly) pointed out, 'has expended little time or resources on the march'. In a revealing insight into Tory thinking, the paper then posed the choice of three basic attitudes to the march and rally:

1. Ignore it [that] [this] would imply that we had no answer: it would be conceding vital territory by default.

2. Ridicule the March as an irrelevant Trotskyist stunt. It is important that the Far Left connections of the March and Rally be brought to the public's attention [...] [but] we must be careful how far we go to deride the Marchers themselves. [...] It may damage our efforts to show ourselves to be a compassionate caring party if we do not respect their efforts.

3. Discredit Labour's right to espouse the cause: The Marchers do not threaten us: Labour does. In the final analysis it does not matter about the Rally, as long as we get re-elected.[15]

The author(s) of the confidential paper need not have worried. The 1983 general election gave the Conservatives one of their best results. Even though they gained 1 per cent fewer votes than in 1979, the Tories won with a massive landslide majority of 144 seats. The Falklands War and the poor showing of Labour helped to account for the Conservative victory. The SDP/Liberal Alliance won 23 seats, but its share of the vote was only 2 per cent less than that of Labour.

Unemployed Workers' Centres (UWCs) and the TGWU

How did the trade union movement react to mass unemployment and consequent membership loss? In 1980, the TUC congress passed a motion 'to consider ways by which the interests of the non-employed could be represented, on the basis that the "social wage" should be a matter for negotiation by Congress, and to report to the next Congress'.[16] It was clear that there were divisions over the best way forward. In 1977, the Newcastle Trades Council established an Unemployed Workers' Centre (UWC). This led to the establishment of many more – 'by May 1981 over 50 Centres, by 1983 over 180 and by 1984 over 200 Centres had been established'.[17] Debates took place as to the purpose of such centres. Were they there to

---

15 Confidential paper, 'Peoples [sic] March for Jobs '83', p.12. Conservative Research Department, 1 June 1983. https://tinyurl.com/43k5da2z.

16 Report of 112th Annual Trades Union Congress, September 1980, p.382.

17 Keith Forrester and Kevin Ward, 'Organising the Unemployed? The TUC and the Unemployed Workers Centres', *Industrial Relations Journal*, 1986, vol.17, no.1, p.48.

act as advice centres or should they attempt to organise the unemployed to oppose government policy? This led to differences of opinion over the question of whether unemployed workers should retain union membership post-redundancy. Maintaining union membership would mean that the unemployed would remain linked to those still in work. The TGWU was clear on both these issues. It was at the forefront of lobbying for the unemployed to retain their union membership and for the UWCs to be campaigning organisations and not merely advice centres. The decisions of the 1981 BDC showed that the TGWU was wholeheartedly in favour of retaining their unemployed sisters and brothers in full and active membership. This was the assurance Alex Kitson (deputy general secretary) gave to one delegate who said that unless the union retained its unemployed members, 'we leave them open to the far right, the fascists of this world, who are already standing outside the school gates'.[18]

The Merseyside 6/612 branch was a good example of the practical operation of the TGWU policy at a local level. Some of its members were prominent in the TGWU at national and regional levels. For example, Bobby Owens, an ex-car worker and leader of the 6/612 branch, was appointed to the post of North West Region secretary in 1985. Following the 1981 People's March for Jobs, the 6/612 branch, together with others, acquired a property in Hardman Street, Liverpool, and opened its doors as a UWC in 1983. In 1984, unemployed users of the UWC in Leeds produced a video in conjunction with TGWU bus workers about the proposed deregulation of public transport and introduced the video at a number of TGWU branches and at Leeds Trades Council.[19]

The Liverpool Hardman Street UWC became one of the largest and most active UWCs and was at the forefront in the battle over another divisive issue: namely, how were UWCs to be funded? The TUC was not averse to accepting government funding via the Manpower Services Commission (MSC).[20] The MSC was a corporatist tripartite body and the TUC was thus represented on its board. However, accepting MSC money came with conditions – UWCs would have to refrain from any kind of political or campaigning activity. Needless to say, the Hardman Street UWC, along with many others, did not accept this poisoned chalice. A debate on this issue was held at the 1987 TGWU BDC. However, an amendment to a motion on UWCs called for a 'financial fund [...] so that the TUC-sponsored centres can be free from financial restraints in campaigning for jobs and an end to unemployment, and to bring the young

18 Quoted in Marren, *We Shall Not Be Moved*, p.86.
19 Information from Forrester and Ward, 'Organising the Unemployed?'
20 The Manpower Services Commission was set up in 1973 to co-ordinate employment and training services in the UK through a ten-member commission drawn from trade unions, employers, local authorities and education. Its training programmes were supposed to alleviate unemployment.

unemployed closer to the trade union and labour movement'.[21] The mover of the amendment clarified that its purpose was explicitly to reject MSC funding. The amendment was lost; nonetheless, the TGWU continued its active support for UWCs and was, according to Ron Todd, the only union to have offered trade union membership to the unemployed at a rate of 10p per week.

The Tory Attack on Trade Unions

Central to Thatcher's strategy was a full frontal attack on trade unions – politically and ideologically. The 'Stepping Stones' Report argued that a Tory victory in the 1979 election must represent

> an explicit rejection of socialism and the Labour-trades unions axis [...] Skilfully handled, however, the rising tide of public feeling could transform the unions from Labour's secret weapon into its major electoral liability.[22]

The 'Stepping Stones' Report even analysed the characteristics of trade union leaders and placed them into three categories:

> [1] Potential allies; forced by national economic failure into short-sighted defence of their members' interests, but knowing that it is economic nonsense. This group has to be persuaded that the Tories have the measure of the UK problem and can cure it, to the benefit of their members.

> [2] Economically confused; well intentioned, but genuinely believe in socialism, government planning, Clause 4, etc. This group must be educated and persuaded that the first group may, after all, be right.

> [3] Political opponents; those who want a true socialist state and will therefore veto any attempts by either party to revive the private sector. This group must, in the public eye, be isolated and discredited, unless their power can be reduced in some other way. For the Tories to treat them as responsible figures, and thus give them increased credibility, must in the end be a mistake.[23]

21 Amendment to motion 188 (Region 1), proposed by Eric Rechnitz, verbatim minutes, 1987 TGWU Biennial Delegate Conference (BDC), Unite archive, Holborn. Rechnitz referenced his involvement in the Hackney UWC.
22 'Stepping Stones' Report, p.S-1.
23 'Stepping Stones' Report, p.14.

The 1981 Report went further when it asked:

> Can a modern democracy afford trade unions as well as a welfare state? Is there a role for trade unions at all? Should we be seeking to make them obsolete, helping them to wither away?[24]

And so the attack on trade unions was launched. Learning the lesson from the defeat of the Heath government's Industrial Relations Act, the Thatcher administration avoided a single comprehensive omnibus assault. Instead, it passed seven separate anti-union laws in the period 1979–1992. The following provides a summary of the legislative attack.

1980: Employment Act

Lawful picketing was restricted to the workers' own place of work. A picketing code of practice limited the number to six pickets. 'Secondary action' was severely restricted. The closed shop was attacked. It required an 80 per cent ballot in favour for approval of its continuance. State funding was offered to finance union ballots. The law giving the right to statutory trade union recognition was repealed. Protections against unfair dismissal and maternity rights were restricted.

1982: Employment Act

Further restrictions on strike action were enacted. This limited industrial action to one's 'own' employer through a redefinition of what constituted a trade dispute. Reversing the 1906 Trades Disputes Act, employers could now obtain injunctions against unions and sue unions for damages as a result of strike action. The 80 per cent ballot rule was extended to all closed shops and balloting was to take place every five years. Generous compensation would be awarded to any worker dismissed due to non-compliance with the closed shop. Union-only labour clauses in commercial contracts were removed. The Act also extended the power of the employer to dismiss strikers or those taking part in industrial action.

1984: Trade Union Act

Elections for trade union executive committees must now be held every five years by secret ballot. Political fund ballots to be held every ten years. The Act redefined the scope of the political objects of trade unions to include expenditure on advertising for a political party or candidate. Secret ballots before industrial action were now mandatory.

---

24 Westwell Report, p.9.

1986: Public Order Act
This introduced new criminal offences in relation to picketing.

1988: Employment Act
Unions were obliged to compensate any member disciplined for non-compliance with majority decisions. Members were now permitted to seek an injunction if a ballot was not held prior to industrial action. Union finances were open to public inspection. Unions were prevented from paying members' or officials' fines for non-compliance with any aspect of employment law. Action to preserve the post-entry closed shop was now deemed unlawful. Further restrictions on industrial action and election ballots were enacted. This included industrial action, which now had to be supported by a majority in a separate ballot in each separate workplace, the ballot paper to include the wording: 'If you take part in strike or other industrial action, you may be in breach of your contract of employment.'

Ballots were now mandatory for non-voting executive members. Election addresses were subject to control by independent scrutiny. Establishment of CROTUM (Commissioner for the Rights of Trade Union Members) to assist any union member who was taking or contemplating taking legal action against his/her union.

1989: Employment Act
Tribunal pre-hearing review and proposed deposit of £150 for cases to be considered by industrial tribunals. Removal of restrictions on the work of women and young workers. Exemption of small employers from providing details of disciplinary procedures. Time off with pay for union duties was now restricted. Written reasons for dismissal now required two years' service.

1990: Employment Act
The Employment Act banned closed shops completely and made it unlawful to refuse to employ non-union members. All secondary action was now deemed unlawful. It widened the circumstances where a union would be liable for its officials' acts. It created extra requirements for a union to repudiate any form of unofficial action. It also imposed extra requirements for union ballots for industrial action and removed unfair dismissal rights for union members participating in unofficial action. The powers of the Trade Union Certification Officer (CO) were extended.

1992: Trade Union and Labour Relations (Consolidation) Act
This brought together all collective employment rights, such as trade union finances and elections; union members' rights, including dismissal, time off, redundancy consultation, the role and functions of ACAS, Central Arbitration Committee (CAC) and CROTUM; and industrial action legislation.

The Trade Union Fightback: Compliance or Defiance?

Following the TUC's conference of trade union executives at Wembley, in 1982, the TGWU launched its own campaign against 'Tebbit's Bill' – later to become law as the 1982 Employment Act (Figure 9). This, the Conservative government's second Employment Act, introduced by the Employment Secretary, Norman Tebbit, in 1982, further restricted the right to take effective industrial action and gave employers the right to dismiss strikers. The Act also undermined union membership agreements and allowed unions to be sued for huge sums in damages.

In 1982, the TUC convened the 'Wembley Conference' of trade union executive committees to rally opposition to the Tory attack on trade unions. It called for non-co-operation with the law and agreed to establish a fund for financial support of unions threatened by court action. The TUC was empowered to organise solidarity for any union threatened with legal action. In addition, the conference pledged to reject state funding of ballots for trade union elections. These laudable decisions, however, were not implemented.

The TGWU published its own detailed plan to resist the provisions of 'Tebbit's Bill', containing a clause-by-clause analysis and proposals for action.[25] Moss Evans's introduction to the pamphlet stated that in his opinion the Tebbit proposals posed an even greater threat to trade unions than Heath's 1971 Act. However, in the changed industrial relations climate, trade union resistance to the 1982 Act and subsequent anti-union legislation did not materialise – a fact wryly observed by a delegate from Region 1 (Bro. J. McGuinness) to the TGWU BDC in 1985: 'Nothing illustrated more the saying of words being cheap with some of the strong speeches and non-existent action from the paper tigers on the Wembley platform.'[26]

Strong feeling against compliance with the law was expressed at the TGWU 1985 BDC. One motion congratulated the union for its 'principled refusal to pay the £200,000 fine imposed for supporting the official strike at British Leyland' but went on to say that the 'policy of passive

---

25 'Tackling Tebbit! A TGWU Guide for Shop Stewards: The Campaign against the 1982 Employment Bill's Attack on Union Rights', TGWU, May 1982.
26 Verbatim minutes, 1985 TGWU BDC, Unite archive, Holborn.

THE GOVERNMENT HAS DECLARED WAR ON TRADE UNIONS

■ They want to smash our agreements about membership with employers.

■ They want to see us dragged into the courts to face penalties of up to a quarter of a million pounds.

■ They want to make outlaws out of people who give assistance to other workers who are in dispute.

■ They want to see workers sacked who refuse to be forced back to work until a dispute is fairly settled.

FIGHT THE GOVERNMENT'S PROPOSALS FOR NEW LEGAL SHACKLES ON THE UNIONS

Published by the Trades Union Congress
Printed by M&C Ltd (TU)

■ The Government's policies have caused soaring unemployment, falling living standards, and drastically reduced social services. Unions are the only defence working people have against the effects of these pernicious policies — that is why the Government wants to weaken us.

■ The TUC will be campaigning against the new legislation proposed by the Secretary of State for Employment. Support the campaign and find out further details of campaign activities from your union.

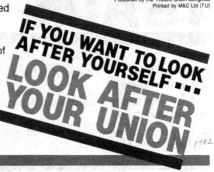

Figure 9: 'If you want to look after yourself ... look after your union':
TUC leaflet opposing 1982 Employment Act
(TUC Library Collections)

non-co-operative [*sic*] is by itself insufficient to defeat the Tory anti-union offensive'.[27] This motion was defeated, as was another that condemned 'those TUC leaders who have failed to support individual trades unions as they have come under attack'. It went on to call for a policy of non-compliance and campaign for a 24-hour general strike in the event of any legal attack.[28]

Todd's reply to the debate, in which he argued for 'flexibility' in response to legal restrictions, was clearly mindful of the TGWU rule book, which permitted only 'lawful' activity. One delegate predicted this response when he admonished 'union bureaucrats' who want 'to use the rule book by saying that we cannot [...] have a strategy of fighting against Tory policy'.[29]

To an extent this was a reversal of the position the union had taken a year earlier in 1984, when, during the National Graphical Association (NGA)–Messenger dispute, the TGWU had backed the call for a one-day solidarity strike. This was in opposition to the TUC position, which, in defiance of the Wembley Conference position, argued that such a solidarity strike would be unlawful.[30] It would therefore seem that the TGWU's call for action to support the NGA in 1984 was a rare anomaly, since the GEC did not call for any similar solidarity action during the year-long miners' strike.

By 1991, the TGWU's attitude to the anti-union laws had changed. The shift in its position was already apparent in 1987 when a motion was passed at the BDC empowering the TGWU to seek government funds for union ballots. The motion argued that in order to protect the union, 'opposition must include a degree of compliance with the law where necessary and a sophisticated tactical approach'.[31] It was argued that this change of policy was justified due to three recent developments, namely

– that in 1986 the TUC decided that whether to apply for [...] Ballot Funds [...] was a matter for the discretion of individual unions;

– that since 1986 ballots on a number of issues have become compulsory by law and all unions have agreed to comply with these provisions;

– that these ballot requirements are bound to involve the union in colossal expenditure year after year.[32]

27 Verbatim minutes, 1985 TGWU BDC, motion 349.
28 Verbatim minutes, 1985 TGWU BDC, motion 362.
29 Verbatim minutes, 1985 TGWU BDC, C. Aherne, Region 1.
30 MRC MSS.787/338. Minutes of the General Executive Committee, 4 June 1984, General Secretary, Quarterly Report.
31 Verbatim minutes, 1987 TGWU BDC, composite motion 44, Unite archive, Holborn.
32 Verbatim minutes, 1987 TGWU BDC, composite motion 44.

A major debate on employment law was held at the 1991 BDC at which it was clear that the spirit of the 'new realism' and Labour's 'third way' politics had impacted on the union's policy decisions. Bill Morris's opening address as the new general secretary-elect recalled that the union had 'suffered a decade of attrition. Two recessions from one government: manufacturing in steep decline and investment at a standstill.'[33] In his reply to the discussion on employment law, he opposed those who insisted on maintaining the union's long-standing policy of calling for the repeal of all Tory anti-union laws, and argued instead for the Labour Party's charter for employment rights as outlined in its 'People at Work' policy document. In this connection he warmly welcomed the European Union's draft social charter. In essence, this meant abandoning the long-standing policy of demanding total repeal of the anti-union legislation because, Morris argued, 'some principles of the present law have a degree of backing'.[34] He cited secret ballots for industrial action and for the election of trade union general secretaries and union executive committees as examples of legal changes which had won support among members and thus should not be repealed. After all, he contended (in an apparent concession to Thatcherite ideology), no one wanted to go back to the bad old days of 1979!

Questions for Discussion

1 How effective was the fight against unemployment?

2 Could trade unions have done more to resist the anti-union legislation?

3 How do you explain the changing attitude to the Tory anti-union laws: should the TGWU have complied with the law?

---

33 Verbatim minutes, 1991 BDC, Unite archive, Holborn.
34 Verbatim minutes, 1991 BDC.

5

The Impact of Thatcherism and the Trade Union Response

Trade Union Membership: Managing Decline

Inevitably, high rates of unemployment and the hostile anti-union environment had a negative impact on trade union membership figures during this period (Figure 10). In common with most trade unions, TGWU membership also fell. In 1979, 53 per cent of workers were union members; by 1998, this had fallen to 30 per cent. In 1980, around 70 per cent of employees' wages were set by collective bargaining; by the mid-1990s, this had sharply fallen to less than 45 per cent. TGWU membership had reached an all-time high of 2 million in 1979 but dropped by 30 per cent to 1,377,944 in 1986 and, even more drastically, declined still further to 858,000 by 2000. Over the same period, the 253,000 members of the National Union of Mineworkers had shrunk to 5,000. Union mergers in the public services were dominated by the creation in 1993 of UNISON. In the private sector, there was a complicated and bewildering set of major mergers. MSF (Manufacturing, Science and Finance) was formed as the result of a merger in 1988 between the Association of Scientific, Technical and Managerial Staffs (ASTMS) and the Technical, Administrative and Supervisory Section (TASS). In 2001, the MSF merged with the Amalgamated Engineering and Electrical Union (AEU) to form Amicus in 2001. Amicus in turn merged/amalgamated with the Graphical Paper and Media Union (GPMU) (1992) in the printing industry and the financial sector union UNIFI (1999). In 2007, Amicus merged with the TGWU to form Unite.

As a result, the number of unions affiliated to the TUC declined from 109 in 1980 (representing 12,172,000 members) to 76 in 2000 (representing 6,746,000). As a union operating primarily in the private sector, the TGWU, like Amicus and the GMB, was particularly exposed to membership decline. In common with other unions, the TGWU sought to stem falling membership by embarking on a course of amalgamation and merger with other unions, which ultimately led to the creation of Unite

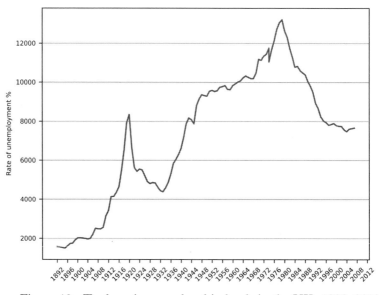

Figure 10: Trade union membership levels in the UK, 1892–2018

the Union in 2007. The genesis of Unite has been termed 'an exemplar of balanced-partner merger' in contrast with the more common process of a 'transfer of engagements'.[1] Although the merger process started in earnest when Bill Morris became general secretary, there were nonetheless 14 amalgamations in the 25 years between 1979 and 2004, resulting in an increase of 129,000 members,[2] the most significant of which was the merger with the National Union of Agricultural and Allied Workers (NUAW) in 1982.

Ron Todd followed Moss Evans as TGWU general secretary (1985–1992) and served for much of the difficult days of the Thatcher era. During this period, the TGWU responded to membership decline and the anti-union environment in several ways, some more successful than others.

TGWU 'Link-Up' Campaign

By the mid-1980s, it was clear that the traditional areas of TGWU strength among male, full-time, permanent employees were in relative (and at times absolute) decline. Equally, it was clear that remedial action was essential. The union responded to some of these changes by launching the 'Link-Up'

---

1 Roger Undy, 'The Making of Unite the Union: The Dynamics of Amalgamation', *Historical Studies in Industrial Relations*, 2018, vol.39, no.39, pp.140–141.
2 Undy, 'The Making of Unite the Union', p.149.

campaign in 1987. This sought to extend trade union organisation to the growing number of hitherto unorganised temporary, part-time and agency workers, the great majority of them women. The campaign raised recruitment to a rate of over 200,000 per year – a major achievement – but one that just about cancelled out membership losses due to redundancies and employer hostility to trade unions.[3] Recruiting new members through the 'Link-Up' campaign undoubtedly yielded short-term results. However, retaining such recruits proved problematic, especially in workplaces where the union was not recognised. 'Link-Up' represented the union's major recruitment initiative of the late 1980s and early 1990s and could be seen as a contribution to the 'organising' as opposed to the 'servicing' strategic model to stem membership decline.[4] However, according to Ed Snape,

> The campaign had failed to halt the decline in membership by the early 1990s. Although there was an increase in numbers recruited, turnover also increased. High turnover has long been recognised as a problem for some unions, but membership losses increased just as Link Up was gathering pace, and officers suggested that this was partly because recruits were often difficult to retain, especially where recognition was lacking.[5]

The Struggle Continues

However, even in this less favourable climate for trade unionism, and despite membership decline, the Thatcher regime was tested by significant opposition in the form of major industrial disputes and community protests. Among the most important of the industrial disputes was the 1984–1985 miners' strike and the Wapping dispute in 1986. The TGWU was involved in both. But these were not the only strikes or industrial disputes. Taken together, however, with the exception of the campaign against the poll tax, Thatcherite strategy outlined in both editions of 'Stepping Stones' was ultimately successful in its principal objective: to shackle the labour movement through draconian legislation, privatising the public sector and creating a hostile ideological climate aimed at crushing socialist values. Needless to say, the mass media (with the exception of the *Morning Star*) were willing and enthusiastic champions of this Tory strategy.

3 Unite the Union, 'The History of the T&G'. www.unitetheunion.org/who-we-are/history/the-history-of-the-tg/.

4 Ed Snape, 'Reversing the Decline? The TGWU's Link Up Campaign', *Industrial Relations Journal*, 1994, vol.25, no.3, pp.222–233.

5 Snape, 'Reversing the Decline?', p.231.

The Poll Tax

Euphemistically termed the Community Charge, the poll tax was a system of local taxation introduced by Margaret Thatcher's government to replace domestic rates in Scotland from 1989, prior to its introduction in England and Wales from 1990. It provided for a single flat rate, per capita tax on every adult, at a figure set by the local authority. Designed to undermine 'the financial and political autonomy of local government',[6] with 'looney left' Labour councils as its main target, the tax was defeated by enormous community mobilisation, mass protest and mass non-payment. Although trade unions and the Labour Party opposed the tax, at national level most unions did not support non-payment. In Scotland, however, the TGWU and the National Communications Union (NCU) supported non-implementation by Labour councils. In 1989, the TGWU debated a carefully worded motion proposed by Les Huckfield (the former Labour MP), condemning the poll tax and calling for

all possible support to those organisations including trade unions, community associations and local authorities in their efforts to resist the Poll Tax, but recognis[ing] that any campaign involving defiance of the law must be part of a mass movement involving the overwhelming support of the people themselves.[7]

The fact that such a mass movement existed did not deter the GEC from opposing the motion on the grounds that it advocated breaking the law. Bill Morris condemned the motion as 'a gift to the Tories'.[8] Unsurprisingly, the motion was defeated.

British Leyland

Early on, the Thatcher plan had identified what it labelled as the most notorious trade union agitators. Top of the list was Derek Robinson, the trade union convenor at British Leyland (BL). The chairman of BL, Michael Edwardes, shared Thatcher's view of 'Red Robbo' and sacked him in November 1979. This sacking marked the first salvo in the Tory attack. Edwardes had been appointed chairman in 1977, two years after the Labour government had taken it into public ownership. Robinson was sacked because in the trade union pamphlet *A Trade Union Response*

---

6 Simon Hannah, *Can't Pay Won't Pay: The Fight to Stop the Poll Tax* (Pluto Press, 2020), p.26.

7 Verbatim minutes, 1989 TGWU BDC, motion 153, Unite archive, Holborn.

8 Verbatim minutes, 1989 TGWU BDC, motion 153.

to the Edwardes Plan, he (among others) called for mass action, including 'work-ins', to prevent the closure of 13 factories that would have resulted in a further 25,000 redundancies in addition to the 18,000 job losses of the previous two years.[9] The TGWU announced official strike action in protest at Robinson's sacking and the mass redundancies. However, this call was not backed by the AUEW, Robinson's union. It is clear that management were aware that the right-wing leadership of the AUEW led by Terry Duffy would not support Robinson, a Communist, and thus refuse to back strike action. This was why Edwardes chose to sack Robinson rather than Jack Adams, a TGWU member and chair of the BL combine committee. In fact, Adams had been primarily responsible for co-ordinating the text of the pamphlet. John Barker, Chairman of the Strike Committee set up by the TGWU Regional Committee, was disgusted by the AUEW action. He said:

We can only deplore the action [the AUEW decision]. It has come as a complete bombshell. It was like the carpet being swept from under our feet. [...] We were elated when we heard the news that our General Secretary had made the dispute official. We could have closed Leyland immediately. Then Moss Evans 'phoned. He was very upset with what had happened. We view the action taken by the engineering union with disgust.[10]

Derek Robinson's sacking was the opening shot – the ferocious anti-union bombardment swiftly followed. As Frank Watters, a Communist Party organiser in the Midlands closely involved in the dispute, recounted:

Longbridge was the first major defeat for the movement after Thatcher's victory in the 1979 General Election and set a tone for things to come. A missed opportunity to secure a victory would have set the Tories thinking. After this came a careful strategy of taking on one by one the big battalions of labour in isolation.[11]

The legal assault on trade unions was, as we have seen, meticulously planned. What remained was the need for the Thatcher to smash the two strongest unions – the miners and the printers – both of which were

9 Information from Graham Stevenson, Andy Chaffer and George Hickman, 'Derek Robinson: A Titan of Trade Unionism Who Never Sold Out', *Morning Star*, 1 November 2017. https://morningstaronline.co.uk/article/derek-robinson-titan-trade-unionism-who-never-sold-out.

10 Quote from Ian Nicholls, 'History: The British Leyland (Motor Corporation Combined) Trade Union Committee – Part Two', AROnline. www.aronline.co.uk/opinion/the-british-leyland-combined-shop-stewards-committee-part-2/.

11 Frank Watters, *Being Frank: The Memoirs of Frank Watters* (Askew Design & Print, 1992).

capable of offering robust resistance to Tory neoliberal economic policy. The miners' strike of 1984–1985 and the Wapping print workers' strike of 1986 both involved the TGWU either directly or in solidarity.

1984 Ford Women

An exception to the subsequent series of trade union defeats in the Thatcher years was the successful equal pay strike of women machinists at Ford Motor Company. The strike in 1968, although often (incorrectly) termed an equal pay strike, was in fact a strike over regrading. Although the deal brokered as a result of the strike increased the women's wages, they did not achieve their original demand to be regraded to the skilled rate (Category C). This point was articulated by Rose Boland, one of the Dagenham machinists' shop stewards. She expressed her disillusionment with the outcome of the 1968 strike, saying, 'although we did get more money, we did not gain the point, we won a battle, but lost the war'.[12]

The women were only regraded into Category C following a further six-week strike in 1984. In 1983, an amendment to the 1970 Equal Pay Act had been passed which permitted equal pay claims not simply if the woman was doing 'the same or broadly similar work' (as per the 1970 Act) but if her work was shown to have 'equal value' in terms of 'effort skill and decision making' to that of a male comparator. The 'equal value' argument was precisely the one that Ford women machinists had always used. However, they did not rely on the law or an industrial tribunal to win their battle; instead, supported by the TGWU, they took industrial action and won (Figure 11). This proved to be a very wise decision since, despite the Julie Hayward v. Cammell Laird case,[13] reliance on the legal process proved to be either lengthy or in most cases futile.

12 Interview with Lil O'Callaghan and Rose Boland by Henry Friedman (1978), quoted in Jonathan Moss, '"We didn't realise how brave we were at the time": The 1968 Ford Sewing Machinists' Strike in Public and Personal Memory', *Oral History*, 2015, vol.43, no.1, p.44.

13 One of the first equal value claims, settled after four years, was brought by Julie Hayward, a qualified cook employed by Cammell Laird in the canteen at their Birkenhead shipyard. Supported by the GMB union, her male co-workers and the Equal Opportunities Commission, she claimed equal pay for work of equal value with several male craft workers. The case went to the House of Lords, where in 1988 she won the right to higher basic pay.

Figure 11:
Protesting TGWU
women

Bus Deregulation: London Fights Back

In line with the privatisation agenda outlined in the Ridley Report, the Thatcher government commissioned a White Paper into the bus industry, culminating in the Transport Act 1985. This was implemented on 26 October 1986, resulting in the deregulation of bus services in England, Scotland and Wales. Deregulation, though, did not apply to London buses, run by London Regional Transport (LRT). In April 1989, however, the buses were split into 11 quasi-independent companies that were privatised in 1994–1995. (The London bus privatisation will be covered in *Unite History*, volume 6.)

The London Bus Section of the TGWU mounted strong opposition to government plans, as is recounted here by Ken Fuller, one of the leading organisers of London Bus Workers. He was a rep at 1/499 Westbourne Park garage (1981–1983), District Officer in the London Bus Section (1983–1995) and Regional Organiser (1995–2003).

Hard Times for London Bus Workers

Ken Fuller

In the post-war years, the prestige of the bus industry declined as passenger numbers fell due to increased car usage and relatively high fares. At the same time, high staff turnover, the decline of left organisation and memories of the failed 1958 strike caused low morale and a lack of confidence in the ability of the London Bus Section to fight its way out of the problems.

On 1 January 1970, responsibility for London Transport (LT) passed to the Greater London Council (GLC). Thereafter, the fortunes of the Section varied according to which party controlled the GLC – and, in the 1980s, the government.

During Labour control of the GLC, from the mid-1970s, fares were held constant, resulting in an increase in passenger mileage. In 1974, the introduction of London weighting, unsocial hours payments and a sizeable increase in basic pay made a major impact on the chronic understaffing situation. When the Tories regained control, fare increases were resumed. Once again, passenger numbers fell, and the Labour government's wage restraint policy reversed the improvement in staff numbers. Attendance at events called by the 'Save Our Buses' campaign was poor, and a motion to ban overtime for a week in mid-1977 to demonstrate the true level of the staff shortage was overwhelmingly defeated.

The Tory GLC then embarked upon a series of service cuts starting with 'Bus Plan 78', which sought to axe scheduled mileage from 211 million miles to 199 million. Opposing this, the TGWU London Bus Section called a number of lightning one-hour strikes, district by district, but the response was less than 100 per cent. Nevertheless, a part of the cuts programme was deferred, pending further discussions. In mid-1978, however, by a margin of a single vote, the union's London Bus Conference accepted the programme. After suffering a £15 million deficit in 1979, London Transport announced further cuts for 1980. A one-hour strike again saw less than total participation.

In May 1981, Labour regained control of the GLC, and, under the leadership of Ken Livingstone, cuts planned for October were scrapped and instead fares on both buses and the Underground were reduced by an average of 32 per cent, resulting in a dramatic rise in passenger numbers, However, following a case brought by Tory-led Bromley council, the Law Lords in December ruled that the fare cuts were unlawful, as LT had a 'fiduciary duty' to attempt to break even. A London Transport Trade Union Defence Committee, uniting all LT unions, was formed, and a one-day strike was declared for 10 March 1982. For the first time ever, buses and Tubes struck together. All over London, large public meetings were held, but the industrial and political wings of the campaign never achieved the degree of unity demanded by the situation; political action was often regarded with cynicism.

The trade union unity demonstrated on 10 March was not maintained, and in the London Bus Section, what was intended to be an open-ended programme of industrial action saw only one token one-hour strike before the demand for negotiations grew. In mid-June, however, nine garages, led by Wandsworth, struck unofficially in support of 32 signalmen on the Underground who were suspended for refusing to feed new rolls into the machine which would operate the reduced schedules. LT agreed to reinstate the men and postpone service cuts while a joint working party investigated alternative ways of making savings. The following month, after LT had agreed to restore 115 of the 785 buses it had planned to cut, a special London Bus Conference voted, by 36 to 27, to accept the cuts.

In addition to the anti-trade union legislation of the Tory government, London bus workers were subjected to a series of vicious Transport Acts. The 1983 Transport Act required the GLC and the Metropolitan Authorities to submit three-year plans on an annual, rolling basis and to put services out to tender where it was thought that the private sector could operate them more cheaply. LT's first three-year plan provided for 6,000 job losses, two-thirds of which would be on the buses, where the reduction would to a significant extent be achieved by accelerated conversion to one-person operation (OPO). Later in 1983, the government published a White Paper in which it announced its intention to remove LT from GLC control, prior to the abolition of the GLC itself, and hand it to an appointed body called London Regional Transport (LRT).

Once again, campaign groups sprang up all over London, and on 28 March 1984 bus and Underground workers held a one-day strike. Given the large Commons majority held by the Tories, however, the LRT Act was passed and the GLC was abolished. In April 1985, the transport undertakings were split into three subsidiaries: London Buses Ltd., Bus Engineering Ltd. and London Underground Ltd.

The 1985 Transport Act provided for the deregulation of bus services elsewhere in the country and the possibility that this could be extended to London, which would entail the anarchy of on-the-road competition on the streets of the capital. As a result of vigorous campaigning by the London Bus Section and public groups, this prospect was avoided.

Initially, private operators won tendered routes because LBL's bids were based on current wages and conditions. The company then put together packages of lower wages and worse conditions without consulting the TGWU. This tactic was first employed at Potters Bar garage, where LBL, having won the tenders, avoided strike action by offering a relatively generous severance package to existing staff. Next time around, it avoided even this by establishing a new low-wage subsidiary called Westlink, which successfully bid for routes operated by the 'mainstream' Hounslow garage just down the road.

A similar exercise was conducted at Orpington, where a small 'midibus' garage was opened.

These developments presented the TGWU with an organisational task, for it now had to ensure that the new workforces at Potters Bar, Westlink and Orpington and the various private operators were brought into the union and integrated into the London Bus Section. While this was eventually accomplished (with the exception of a handful of small private operators), it was not without its problems, for a considerable body of opinion within the mainstream LBL membership tended to look upon the members at the low-wage subsidiaries as poor relations and those working for private operators as the 'enemy'. In effect, members who acted in this way were more loyal to their employer than to their class – a further example of how the consciousness of the Section had deteriorated.

Nevertheless, such problems were overcome by a variety of means. Morale was improved by the adoption of a combative stance whenever possible and vigorous public campaigning against deregulation. In addition, in the early 1980s, a group of activists produced an unofficial publication called *London Busworker* (this had started life as the branch newsletter at the new Westbourne Park garage), thousands of copies of which were sold to the branches every month. Then again, the TGWU took the lead in the formation of transport campaigns in west and north London.

Route-tendering gave rise to two major disputes, and the tactics adopted by the membership in each of these was radically different. The first occurred at Norbiton garage, just outside Kingston, where the incumbent LBL won the tenders based on worsened wages and conditions. Initially, the stance adopted by the London Bus Committee, supported by the Norbiton membership, was that there should be no negotiations, as the fleet agreement should be defended at all costs. But where would such a stance lead? Eventually, LRT would withdraw the routes from Norbiton and award them to Len Wright Travel, which, although it came second in the bidding, paid even lower wages. Eventually, common sense prevailed, and negotiations, backed by strike action, were renewed, and after several improvements to the original proposals, the membership reluctantly voted to accept.

By the time of the second dispute, in July 1991, LBL had been split into 13 operating subsidiaries, of which London Forest Travel (LFT) was one. When the company retained the tendered routes at Walthamstow garage, its directors were jubilant, but then announced that deep cuts in earnings and longer hours would be necessary – not just at Walthamstow but also at Ash Grove, Clapton and Leyton. A repeat of Norbiton? Not at all, because the union knew that the company which had come second in the bidding for the largest block of routes – Citybus – was offering a package superior to LFT's proposals. The membership therefore agreed to a strategy in which strike action would be maintained until LFT came up with a package which at least equalled that offered by

Citybus. It was realised, of course, that if agreement could not be reached LRT would reassign the routes to Citybus, the managing director of which had promised recognition of the TGWU in such an event.

Early on, LFT agreed to restrict its proposals to Walthamstow garage – but then refused to give an undertaking that its outrageous proposals would not in future be applied to the other three garages, thus allowing the union to lawfully include them in the strike ballot, which saw a very high turnout and a massive affirmative vote. LFT never equalled the rates proposed by Citybus, and the strike therefore lasted for 19 days, making it the longest London bus strike since 1958. Throughout the dispute, morale was extremely high, buoyed by the support offered by the public, widespread media coverage and a message of support from the union's Biennial Delegate Conference, then meeting in Blackpool. LFT activists lived up to the name, manning a strike office in Walthamstow, sending collectors out to the public and, every Friday, to bus garages across London. In all, over £60,000 was received in donations.

As predicted, LRT withdrew the tendered routes from LFT and offered them to Citybus. LBL then closed its LFT subsidiary completely, allocating the remaining routes and two of the garages to neighbouring subsidiaries Leaside and East London. In addition, rather than releasing fully trained surplus staff to its private competitor, LBL agreed to accommodate all staff who wished to remain in its network, with the others receiving the LBL severance package.

It could be said, therefore, that London bus workers ended this period on something of a high note. Although wages and conditions had still taken a hit, the outrageous London Forest proposals had been soundly defeated and morale was greatly improved. The London Forest dispute could have proved a model for dealing with incumbent employers who chose to win tenders at the expense of their workers.

The Miners' Strike, 1984–1985

The heroic struggle of British miners to save their industry and their communities, culminating in their year-long strike, was precipitated by the Tory government's determination to crush the NUM. A top secret 74-page document written in 1981 by the government's Central Policy Review Staff (CPRS) assessed what it termed the 'balance of power' between the NUM and the government and what could be done to tilt it in the government's favour.[14] It argued that NUM power was based on their

14 The Central Policy Review Staff (CPRS), nicknamed the 'Think-Tank', was an independent unit within the Cabinet Office. See CPRS Study of the 'NCB/ NUM Problem', 18 July 1981, The National Archives, PREM19/854 f175. www. margaretthatcher.org/source/prem19/prem19-0854.

unique support within their own communities and the solidarity which other unions and the public in general traditionally showed to the miners. This was coupled with the fact that the NUM had a stranglehold on the economy because 75 per cent of Britain's energy came from coal-fired power stations. The report offered several solutions to break the power of the union. This included increasing coal stocks, importing foreign coal together with establishing coastal coal-based power stations and promoting nuclear power. The report also noted that 12 per cent of British coal came from open cast mines and that workers in them were TGWU members. The report thus proposed that these open cast mines be moved to the private sector. The CPRS report acknowledged that the internal affairs of the NUM were closely monitored – presumably by Special Branch. It advocated that the government's aim should be to break the unity of the union in an effort to isolate the militant supporters of Arthur Scargill, who it was feared would succeed the moderate Joe Gormley.[15] Nottinghamshire, the report presciently noted, was a moderate area and could thus be relied upon to oppose Scargill-inspired future militancy, thereby creating NUM disunity. Such was the carefully crafted Tory strategy.

The TGWU and the Miners' Strike

The TGWU gave unconditional support to the miners from the outset. In his quarterly report to the GEC, Moss Evans had stated that he had attended the first joint meeting of a putative version of a resurrected triple (potentially quadruple) alliance of miners (NUM), road transport (TGWU), rail (NUR and ASLEF) and seamen (NUS).[16] He reported that TGWU members working in open cast mines had withheld coal supplies and that the union centrally had donated £30,000 in addition to substantial support from the regions of the TGWU. The policy of the union was clearly stated as 'not moving coal or coke, or oil substituted for coal or coke, across NUM official picket lines'.[17]

In April 1984, the National Co-ordinating Committee of Transport Unions and the NUM published national guidelines to set out the

---

15 It was later revealed by the BBC in the 2002 'True Spies' television series that the former NUM chief was a Special Branch informant. http://news.bbc.co.uk/1/hi/programmes/true_spies/2351547.stm.

16 MRC MSS.787/338. Minutes of the General Executive Committee, 4 June 1984, General Secretary, Quarterly Report, Appendix I. The triple alliance is a reference to the alliance of road, rail and mining unions, first formed in 1914, and reactivated in 1919 and 1921 to support locked-out miners. See *Unite History*, volume 1.

17 Minutes of the General Executive Committee, 4 June 1984, General Secretary, Quarterly Report, Appendix I.

conduct the union expected of transport workers during the miners' strike. This sought to clarify the agreed policy of 'no movement of coal or coal products into or out of the country nor internally within the country unless by prior agreement with the NUM'.[18] The policy listed a number of permitted dispensations, the most challenging of which for the TGWU was that relating to industries dependent on coal or coke products to be transported from foundries and steel works. Deliveries by road transport of such products were to be permitted only for the purpose of maintenance of those plants in order to avoid their permanent closure, but it was not to be permitted 'for the purposes of continued production during the dispute'. Despite the tough wording, this clause was honoured more in the breach than the observance. It was clear from the outset that there was a conflict of interest between the NUM and the unions representing steel workers and foundry workers. Reg Preston, the general secretary of the National Union of Domestic Appliance and General Metal Workers (NUDAGMW) complained that if TGWU lorry drivers refused to handle coking coal, his members' jobs would be at risk. In July 1984, the steel committee unions issued a press statement which said that while they had great sympathy for the miners, it would nonetheless 'not be practicable to accede to the NUM's request that [...] all production of steel should cease forthwith'.[19]

Lorry Drivers and the Miners' Strike

As far as the guidelines were concerned, the attitude of the non-transport unions was insignificant compared with that of strike-breaking haulage firms, many of whose drivers were TGWU members. As expected, the TGWU, in accordance with the national guidelines, instructed its lorry driver members not to cross NUM picket lines. In the expectation of compliance with this instruction, the TGWU's national Road Transport (Commercial) (RTC) trade group declared to the employers that it would 'not tolerate any "victimisation" of lorry drivers involved in or affected by the miners' dispute'[20] and that the union would support (including financially) any member who was suspended from work for adhering to union policy. However, it soon became clear that lorry drivers were not obeying the union's instructions. The RTC trade group journal *The Highway* reported that the RTC had called for 'the immediate regional investigation into the breaches of miners' picket lines by lorry drivers'.[21] It warned that if 'following investigation drivers who are members of

18   MRC MSS.126/TG/1395/5/1.
19   MRC MSS.126/TG/1395/5/1.
20   *The Highway*, May 1984.
21   *The Highway*, August 1984.

the union can be identified then consideration should be given by the Regional Committee concerned to exclusion from union membership'. Clearly, most members were not following the example set in South Wales where TGWU haulage drivers' leader Geoff Jacob reported that his members fully supported the miners' strike. He explained that this was due to their strong identity with the miners because his lorry driver members lived in the same community. As a result of their solidarity action, a thousand of his members were out of work. Jacob commented:

> The hauliers who do not live and work in South Wales do not understand the problems that exist. You have to live in a mining community to understand [...] The NUM is a good ally for haulage drivers, and will continue to be. The miners' dispute has to do with both dockers and drivers. [...] You cannot be a fair weather trade unionist.[22]

Plainly, this adherence to trade union principles was lacking elsewhere and this led to bitter recriminations. Dennis Skinner MP sent Moss Evans a 35-page dossier listing hundreds of strike-breaking haulage firms. This information was regularly updated. It was clear that TGWU members, despite exhortation and instruction, had failed to abide by the national guidelines. In March 1985, when the miners' strike was over, the GEC, somewhat belatedly, expressed its concern about 'the transportation of coal during the dispute' and decided to conduct an investigation.[23]

It would thus seem that the Ridley Report's strategy of getting 'some haulage companies to recruit non-union drivers who will be prepared to cross picket lines'[24] had been successful. This was unsurprising given that Ridley himself was Secretary of State for Transport during the miners' strike. In this capacity, Ridley was delighted to reassure the prime minister 'that the recruitment of non-union haulage firms had been a success, and that "virtually all coal (was) being delivered"'.[25] What gave the government even greater pleasure was the fact that trade union members were prepared to cross NUM picket lines.

22 'What the Strike Means to Hauliers', 25 August 1984. https://archive.commercial-motor.com/article/25th-august-1984/28/what-the-strike-means-to-hauliers.

23 'What the Strike Means to Hauliers'.

24 Economic Reconstruction Group, 'Final Report of the Economic Reconstruction Group' (Ridley Report), p.26. Margaret Thatcher Foundation, Personal and Party Papers, Thatcher MSS (2/6/1/37). www.margaretthatcher.org/document/110795.

25 Phil Rawsthorne, 'Implementing the Ridley Report: The Role of Thatcher's Policy Unit during the Miners' Strike of 1984–1985', *International Labor and Working-Class History*, 2018, vol.94, p.175.

Dockers and the Miners' Strike

Two national dock strikes were called in 1984. Both were related to support for the miners' strike, but the spark for both was the ongoing attempt by the port employers, supported by the Tory government, to undermine the National Dock Labour Scheme.[26] In July, a 12-day national dock strike took place. The National Docks Committee of the TGWU called the strike because the British Steel Corporation (BSC) had used workers who were not registered dockers to unload iron ore at Immingham dock on the Humber. The ore was bound for the Scunthorpe steel works and had been blacked by Immingham dockers in support of the miners. This strike was not solid – it was supported by registered dock workers (RDWs) in National Dock Labour Scheme (NDLS) ports only. The 13,000 registered dockers in the NDLS ports stopped work as soon as the strike was called, but the major non-NDLS ports (around 22,000 dockers were outside the scheme), such as Felixstowe, Harwich and Newcastle, carried on working. This was followed by a second national dock strike in support of miners in 1984. The issue was similar to the first strike in that it was sparked by a protest against the unloading of the coal ship *Ostia* by non-registered dock workers at Hunterston dock. The coal was destined for the Ravenscraig steel plant. Although an agreement had been reached by the NUM with the BSC that 18,500 tonnes of coal would be delivered to Ravenscraig in order to maintain minimum operations and safety standards, the BSC broke the agreement. In doing so they used non-registered dock labour to move the coal, thereby precipitating the strike. The TGWU strike spread quickly to major Scottish ports, including Aberdeen, Dundee and Leith. Nicholas Ridley, Secretary of State for Transport, was clear, albeit mistakenly, that the dock strikes had nothing to do with the employers' contravention of the NDLS, but that 'dockers are deciding to join the miners' strike for political reasons'.[27]

Hence it seemed initially that the dockers might have opened a possible 'second front' in support of the miners. However, this did not materialise because, according to Ralph Darlington, it was unknown for dockers to picket other dockers – it had never been necessary, such was the degree of solidarity.[28] Nonetheless, for reasons not fully explained, 'striking dockers could no longer rely on this sort of "automatic solidarity" possibly even

---

26 The NDLS was abolished in 1989. This is discussed at pp.82–84 of the present volume.

27 Hansard, HC vol.63, cols 879–886 (22 May 1981). https://api.parliament.uk/historic-hansard/commons/1984/jul/10/dock-strike.

28 Ralph Darlington, 'There is No Alternative: Exploring the Options in the 1984–5 Miners' Strike', *Capital and Class*, 2005, vol.29, no.3, pp.71–95. https://usir.salford.ac.uk/id/eprint/10099/3/1972_and_1984_Miners%2527_Strikes.pdf.

less than the miners could'.[29] In practice, this turned out to be the case. Within a few days, the dock strike collapsed. In fact, it is more likely that the possibility of a second front might have been opened by the lorry drivers. But, as we have seen, this too did not materialise.

According to Len McCluskey, the dockers' 'second front' failed to materialise because 'there was no strategic leadership', and this in turn was exacerbated by both the failure of the TUC and the weakness of the left, including the Communist Party.[30] McCluskey's opinion tends, therefore, to give credence to the view, expressed by Darlington, that

> The first dockers' strike in July 1984, in particular, potentially transformed the miners' situation given that, although defeated at Orgreave, with other trade unionists joining them out on strike they could still have won. [...] Coal Board chairman Ian MacGregor acknowledged that the widening-out of the strike to the docks 'caused a great deal of anxiety' inside BSC and the government, and demonstrated the 'tightrope we had to walk all the time to keep the miners' strike from becoming a national trade-union issue'. In the event, the hesitation and inaction of the TGWU leadership contributed to the strike's collapse, as what had begun as a show of strength ended in failure.[31]

Thus it was that the TGWU's 'unconditional support' for the miners' strike was expressed more in terms of generous financial support than the kind of practical solidarity expected by the NUM. In this connection, the failure to prevent lorry drivers from crossing NUM picket lines and the collapse of the dock strike were bitter disappointments to the miners. It was also a disappointment to the leadership of the TGWU, which had expected more from their members.

After a bitter year-long battle, faced with the full force of both the repressive and ideological apparatus of the state, the miners' strike ended in March 1985. The NUM's finances were now under the control of the Official Receiver, a fact which Moss Evans reported to the GEC in July 1985. Direct financial support to the NUM by a 'third party' would, Evans said, be ruled as 'contempt of court' and thus, to avoid a legal challenge, a suitably vague commitment pledging continued (financial) support was to be left in the hands of the executive officers 'to give appropriate assistance'.[32] Evans also reported that he had attended a post-strike

29 Sam Fanto, 'So Near – So Far: A History of the British Miners, Part 1', Dialectical-Delinquents   (2005).   https://dialectical-delinquents.com/articles-chronologically-2/class-struggle-histories-2/uk/so-near-so-far-a-history-of-the-british-miners/.
30 Interview with Len McCluskey, 27 January 2022, Unite Oral History Archive.
31 Darlington, 'There is No Alternative', pp.87–88.
32 MRC MSS.787/339. Minutes of the General Executive Committee, 1985.

Miners' Support meeting at Wrexham, where it emerged that he had a clear difference of opinion with Arthur Scargill's demand that a future Labour government should pledge itself to grant an amnesty for all miners convicted during the dispute. Evans was opposed to this and called instead for the reinstatement of sacked miners and for a full judicial review of the sentences of imprisoned miners, 'on the basis that the sentences during the dispute reflected the political dogma of the judiciary'.[33]

According to Len McCluskey, two factors hampered effective solidarity with the miners by the TGWU.[34] One was the clause in the TGWU's rule book which obliged the union to work within the law. (This clause was removed from the Unite Rule Book in 2015.) The second (and arguably more significant) factor was, in McCluskey's view, the lack of clear strategic leadership in the TGWU and the entire labour movement. This in turn was due to the decline and retreat of the left and the ideological dominance of 'new realism' within the labour movement (including the Communist Party) in the face of the Thatcherite onslaught.

Wapping: 'Fire and Hire'

The miners' defeat was followed by a broader employer offensive to radically worsen established terms and conditions of employment in other industries, especially where union strength through collective bargaining had resulted in good contracts of employment for workers. The historical strength of the print unions in winning decent terms and conditions for their members was one such example. Thus the print unions, with very high rates of union membership in most large workplaces, were (as in the case of the NUM) a target for both government and employers in their twofold aim of crushing union strength and maximising profit by reducing wages and degrading working conditions. The miners' strike and the Wapping dispute showed just how much the balance of power had swung to business and government in the Thatcher years. 'Wapping revealed the extent to which ruthless employers could move with relative impunity against workers and their organisations.'[35]

In 1986, 5,500 national newspaper workers at the Rupert Murdoch-owned News International group struck over mass redundancies. This followed the introduction of new technology and the termination of collective agreements for the surviving workforce. It resulted in the dismissal of all the strikers at four national newspapers – *The Sun*, the *Sunday Times*,

---

33 Minutes of the General Executive Committee, 1985.
34 Interview with Len McCluskey.
35 Keith Ewing, 'Solidarity Must Triumph over Unjust Labour Laws', *Morning Star*, 23 January 2016. https://morningstaronline.co.uk/a-4ed2-solidarity-must-triumph-over-unjust-labour-laws-1.

The Times and the *News of the World*. As revealed in a letter leaked to the *Morning Star*, this was a calculated strategy by the employer. News International's lawyers made this clear. 'Dismissing a man on strike has a number of advantages – he will not be entitled to a redundancy payment or to bring a claim for unfair dismissal.'[36]

Labour laws then in force thus enabled the company to relocate with impunity, and to start afresh with a replacement workforce. The replacement workforce was supplied and recruited by the Electrical, Electronic, Telecommunications and Plumbing Union (EEPTU). In fact, since the summer of 1985, Murdoch, in secret collaboration with Frank Chapple, the leader of the EEPTU, had already begun to recruit a workforce to be located at the newly built Wapping plant. It was falsely claimed that the new technology installed in the Wapping plant was for production of the *London Post*, a new evening paper, rather than all the existing titles. As one of the Society of Graphical and Allied Trades (SOGAT) strikers put it:

> At the extreme end of the emerging 'partnership with the employers' vogue, the electricians' union, the EETPU, had connived with the company to recruit and train an entire substitute workforce to operate equipment at the site in east London which had been developed originally to be staffed by the unionised workforce. The EETPU was forced out of the TUC for their treachery two years after the strike was declared at an unsuccessful end.[37]

Much to the dismay of the print unions and the TGWU, this anti-union, employer-collaborationist action of the EEPTU was met only with a mild rebuke by the TUC. Ron Todd, in his quarterly statement to the General Council, reported that under rule 13, the TUC had merely asked, not instructed, the EEPTU to 'cease these damaging activities'. Shock was expressed that the union was not expelled. The NGA's call for its expulsion at the 1986 TUC congress had been ruled out of order, but a motion calling for the TUC to instruct the EEPTU to stop scabbing was passed. However, in November of that year, the TUC General Council voted to ignore this instruction. It was clear to most trade unionists that the EEPTU had blatantly defied the Bridlington Agreement and that this amounted to a prima facie case for expulsion.[38] Two years later, the

---

36 Ewing, 'Solidarity Must Triumph over Unjust Labour Laws'.
37 Ann Field, 'The Tory Attack on Trade Unions', in Mary Davis (ed.), *A Centenary for Socialism: Britain's Communist Party* (Manifesto Press, 2020).
38 In 1939, the Bridlington congress adopted a series of recommendations designed to minimise disputes between unions over membership questions. They laid down the procedures by which the TUC dealt with complaints by one organisation against another and considered disputes between unions. This was formalised into the Bridlington Principles which were set out in the booklet *Relations Between Unions*.

Figure 12: 'The truth behind the barbed wire: Don't buy *The Sun,
News of the World, The Times*'
(TUC Library Collections)

EEPTU was expelled for a minor misdemeanour, entirely unrelated to
its reprehensible anti-union behaviour during the News International
dispute.

The sacked print workers started to picket the strike-breaking EEPTU
workforce at the gates of the fortified Wapping Factory and at the
News International plant at Kinning Park in Glasgow. Mass pickets and
demonstrations were organised to try to stop the speeding TNT jugger-
naut lorries bringing papers out of the plant. Hundreds and sometimes
many thousands of supporters turned out on Wednesday and Saturday
nights for the whole year of the strike. Elsewhere, workers at wholesale
distribution depots in London refused to handle Murdoch's papers.
Supporters picketed wholesalers and TNT depots to stop trucks delivering
papers and the so-called 'white mice' vans taking them out to newsagents.
However, within two days of the strike being declared and the workers
being dismissed, injunctions had been issued to four unions to stop all
forms of solidarity action. In practice, this meant restraining unions from
instructing or allowing their members to refuse to handle or deal with
anything coming out of the Wapping site. SOGAT, which had already
instructed members at wholesale depots not to handle News International
titles, thus found itself in contempt of court and had its entire funds
seized by the courts. Injunctions were also issued against the National

Graphical Association (NGA), against the Union of Communication Workers (UCW) – which was refusing to distribute *Sun* bingo cards – and against the TGWU – which had instructed its drivers not to cross picket lines at News International (Figure 12).

The Role of the TGWU at Wapping

Soon after the sacked workers at News International established their picket lines at Wapping, the TGWU instructed their lorry driver members employed by TNT and other driver members not to cross the SOGAT/NGA picket lines. A two-sided leaflet was distributed to members.[39] The first side consisted of a letter signed by Ron Todd condemning Murdoch's 'dictatorial methods'. It continued on a personal note:

> From my own involvement in this matter, I am quite convinced by the facts and history of this dispute that News International has sought to use our own union members, outside legitimate agreements. [...] This has convinced me that it is proper and necessary to instruct all TGWU member drivers in TNT and any other firms which are or may become involved not to cross picket lines.

The second side of the leaflet, entitled 'Facts about the Dispute', expounded the SOGAT/NGA case in detail and explained that a victory for Murdoch would have disastrous implications for the future of trade unionism, since the dispute was about 'union busting'. The role and protection of lorry drivers was clarified. Members were told (in bold type following a starred bullet point) that the TGWU 'has an agreement with TNT that no disciplinary action will be taken if you refuse to cross a picket line'. Drivers were asked not to 'fall for the line that your action won't make any real difference', citing the refusal of the BRS truck rental drivers the previous year to cross *Daily Mirror* picket lines. This, it said, was an action which 'helped to bring Robert Maxwell back to genuine negotiations'.

However, by March 1986, it was clear that the appeal to TNT drivers to support trade union principles was unsuccessful. In a circular to regional secretaries and branches responsible for TNT membership, Ron Todd expressed his condemnation of drivers' failure to abide by the demands of their union:

> Drivers employed by TNT who are in membership of the TGWU have played a critical role in supporting Murdoch by continuing

---

39 See www.marx-memorial-library.org.uk/project-type/wapping-dispute.

to cross the official picket lines established by the print unions at Wapping despite an instruction not to do so. [...] The action of the drivers concerned has brought the good name of our union into disrepute.[40]

A conference of TNT reps was convened in April as a 'final appeal' to reverse the situation. It was unsuccessful, and as a consequence of their strike-breaking action in the Wapping dispute Ron Todd expelled 32 TNT lorry driver members from the TGWU.

Given the level of police violence, the pernicious role of the scab EEPTU and the draconian effects of the anti-union legislation, it is hardly surprising that on 8 May 1987, after almost a year of struggle and seques-tration, SOGAT purged its contempt and instructed members to stop blacking News International. The dispute was over.

UNITE's former general secretary, Len McCluskey, acknowledged the defeat at Wapping, but urged that political lessons be drawn from it:

We must take inspiration from the struggle at Wapping, not to look backwards mournfully, but to redouble our efforts to organise to win from the Labour Party a firm commitment to introduce a new framework of employment law and trade union rights fully compliant with our international treaty obligations, particularly ILO Conventions 87 and 98, on the right to organise, the right to bargain collectively and the right to strike.[41]

Questions for Discussion

1 How do you account for the defeats of the miners' strike and the Wapping dispute, despite the fact that both disputes attracted mass support?

2 What was the role of the TGWU in both disputes?

3 What can now be learned from the way the Conservatives planned their attack on the trade union movement?

---

40 Circular dated 18 March 1986. Copy kindly supplied by Ann Field, curator of the Printers' Collection at Marx Memorial Library. www.marx-memorial-library.org.uk/special-collections-and-subject-guides/printers-collection.

41 See www.marx-memorial-library.org.uk/project-type/wapping-dispute.

6

The 'Forward March' of Labour Halted?

Weathering the Storm: Managing Decline and Internal Dissention

Defeats in major industrial disputes, continued decline in union membership and the seemingly unstoppable triumph of Thatcherism impacted negatively on the labour movement in the period 1985–1992 and beyond. This, and the Tories' third election victory in 1987, precipitated a widespread acceptance in the labour movement of the need to accommodate socialist politics and industrial relations to the new reality. The 'third way', and later 'New realism'/'New Labour', was the Labour Party's answer, Eurocommunism was the Communist Party's response, and social partnership was the strategy proffered by the leadership of the trade union movement. Redolent, albeit in different circumstance, of the 'defence not defiance' slogan of mid-1850s 'new model unions' and of 'Mondism' (the post-1926 variant of social partnership),[1] the TUC, at its annual congress in 1983, advocated a collaborative partnership with the employers, in contrast to an adversarial model. This chimed with the new and widely adopted employer strategy of Human Resource Management (HRM). John Kelly describes HRM as a 'counter-mobilization against organized labour' in which the employee is seen as 'the employer's most valued asset whose talents and motivation can be harnessed to corporate goals that will benefit both parties to the employment relationship. In this world view, ideas of conflicting interests are rhetorically castigated as old-fashioned and irrelevant throwbacks to the past.'[2]

Many trade union leaders shared this 'new realist' view. For them, the defeat of the miners and the printers had shown that the labour versus capital confrontational version of industrial relations was now untenable and out of date and that, in the light of the second and third Conservative

---

1 'Mondism' is fully examined in *Unite History*, volume 1.

2 John Kelly, *Rethinking Industrial Relations: Mobilization, Collectivism and Long Waves* (Routledge, 1998), p.129.

election victories, waiting for a Labour government to sort things out was a vain hope. When a Labour victory came at last, in 1997, it should have come as no surprise that Prime Minister Tony Blair announced that the unions could only expect 'fairness, not favours'. After all, it was 'New Labour', with Tony Blair at the helm, which had already pioneered the ideology of the 'third way' politics of new realism and, as a result, signalled its departure from socialist principles in 1995, when Clause 4 was rewritten and the 'third way' became the new mantra.

Jane Holgate observes that, based on the 'new realist' ideological mantra, trade unions adopted one of a range, or in some cases a combination, of strategic models in this period.[3] One strategy was the EEPTU's policy of pursuing single-union agreements and no-strike deals. Although this was not widely favoured by other unions, it was not rejected by the TUC itself. Its 1984 policy statement implied acceptance of no-strike deals in return for closer working with employers on all matters of common interest. This was more fully spelled out in 1991 in *A New Agenda: Bargaining for Prosperity in the 1990s*, which highlighted the need for unions to offer more individual, as opposed to collective, services to members.[4] This approach, it said, should encompass both the bargaining agenda and also the offer of improved services to individual members as part of their union subscription. On the bargaining front, such issues as training, job satisfaction and job security were seen as pragmatic and collaborative non-confrontational issues fostering social partnership. Within the union itself, a similar individualistic approach was advocated and endorsed in practice by most unions. Members were offered a range of services like cheap insurance, free legal advice and good deals on cars and holidays. Taken together, these offerings have become known as the top-down 'servicing model' predicated on the managerialist assumption that members are basically a passive force who, like customers, want to have things done *for* them rather than *by* them. This is well expressed by John Kelly and Ed Heery, who wrote that managerial trade unionism sees members as 'reactive consumers whose needs must be constantly tracked and responded to by unions drawing on the techniques of strategic management'.[5] Other strategies, adopted by the TGWU among others, included new recruitment policies (such as the 'Link-Up' campaign) and mergers with other unions.

The Labour Party policy review of 1987, following its third election defeat, ushered in what effectively became New Labour, before Blair used it as a designation when he became Labour leader in 1994 following the death of John Smith. Thus New Labour was a product of a decade spent

---

3 Jane Holgate, *Arise: Power, Strategy and Union Resurgence* (Pluto Press, 2021).

4 GMB and Union of Communication Workers, *A New Agenda: Bargaining for Prosperity in the 1990* (GMB, 1991). Based on the work of the then GMB secretary, John Edmonds.

5 Quoted in Holgate, *Arise*, p.122.

remaking the Labour Party. That decade began with the then Labour Party leader, Neil Kinnock, initiating a sweeping policy review, which ushered in the 'third way' political programme. The battle over the policy review reached a climax in 1988 when Tony Benn challenged Kinnock for the leadership of the party. After Kinnock won, the influence of the left wing of the party declined and those in favour of the policy review pressed rapidly ahead.[6] The review advocated an abandonment of traditional Keynesian economic theory in favour of supply-side economics. Developed in the 1970s, supply-side economic theory was based on strategies to increase competitiveness and free-market efficiency. It entailed the introduction of measures which undoubtedly, whether intended or not, were to have a damaging impact on trade union policy and practice. The supply-side economic orthodoxy involved three essential elements: a reduction in the role of the state through such measures as privatisation and deregulation, lower income tax rates, and reduced power of trade unions. The Tories had already adopted such policies – they had been pioneered in the United States under President Reagan, sometimes known as 'Reaganomics'. What was new, and shocking to the socialist left, however, was the adoption of such policies by the Labour Party. In a further rebuff to the left, the party abandoned unilateralism. In addition, it also reduced the power of the trade unions within the party's internal structures by decreasing their voting share in the selection of MPs and election to the party's National Executive Committee.

Labour, the 'Third Way', Ron Todd and the TGWU

Throughout their history, the relationship between the TGWU and the Labour Party has always been of the utmost importance. As an affiliate, and the biggest union in Britain, the TGWU had always been the most important financial and political backbone of the Labour Party. The relationship (as previous volumes in this series have shown) was often fraught, especially during the Wilson/Callaghan government. It was tested again in this period when, following its defeat in the 1987 general election, the Labour Party launched its policy review. Ron Todd, as general secretary, was highly critical. His views were expressed in a series of revealing handwritten, diary-style notes, possibly not intended for public consumption.[7] In 1988, he gives us an insight into what turned out to be a very controversial speech that he delivered at a *Tribune* rally held at the Labour Party conference of that year. In a clear reference to the ongoing policy review, he outlined what he saw

---

6 Mark Bevir, 'The Remaking of Labour, 1987–1997', *Observatoire de la société britannique*, 2009, vol.7. http://journals.openedition.org/osb/861.

7 Ron Todd Archive, MRC MSS.572/39.

as two rival positions – the 'modernisers' and the 'nostalgics'. The former were 'all sharp suits, cordless phones, clipboards and scientific samples who know that style and presentation is important, but let political substance pass them by'. The 'nostalgics', on the other hand, 'look back to a misty past which never existed. For them the history of the Labour Movement was a long and glorious record of Proletarian foot soldiers sold out by the rotten leadership.'[8] Todd then went on to outline his own position, which essentially was articulated by him as 'a plague on both your houses'. He wanted a Labour government to be elected not on a purely anti-Thatcher vote but because 'people recognised the need for a fundamental change in political thought based on Democratic Socialism'.

This speech provoked a tremendous (and for Todd unexpected) furore. Todd was shunned by his supposed now erstwhile comrades. He reports that the only person who spoke to him after the speech was, surprisingly, Dennis Healey. Of greater significance was the vitriolic press coverage Todd and his speech received. He was not surprised by the attitude of the Tory press, but the venom of Maxwell's *Daily Mirror* was the worst, and shocked him the most. The *Mirror*'s editorial stated: 'There is no future in the Labour Party for people like Ron Todd who want to live in the past.'[9] The paper then went on to set up a phone vote for readers to choose between Neil Kinnock and Ron Todd as to who best represents the Labour Party – obviously heavily tilted to the former. When, in the 1992 general election, Labour was again defeated, Todd ironically noted that the *Daily Mirror* had changed its line. Now it blamed Labour's defeat on its reliance on 'slick broadcasts and smart suits' instead of 'grassroots commitment and passionate campaigning'.[10] Precisely the issue he had in raised in 1988 and for which he had been vilified.

For Todd, 1988 was a year of 'internal intrigue in Labour Party'.[11] The policy review was completed and had resulted in the abandonment of the socialist policies which Todd held dear and which had been championed by the TGWU for many years. He listed these reversals thus:

- Labour Party now supports the sale of council houses
- Europe is now answer to all our prayers
- Unilateralism abandoned
- Close links with trade unions now an embarrassment
- General watering down of socialist principles.[12]

8 Ron Todd Archive, MRC MSS.572/39.
9 Quoted by Todd, Ron Todd Archive, MRC MSS.572/39.
10 Ron Todd Archive, MRC MSS.572/39.
11 Ron Todd Archive, MRC MSS.572/39. Todd also refers in the same document to internal intrigue in the TGWU. This is outlined at pp.80–81 of the present volume.
12 Ron Todd Archive, MRC MSS.572/39.

TGWU: Weathering the Storm

A bleak prospect for the labour movement, but was its 'forward march' irredeemably halted in this period of retrenchment? How did the TGWU weather the storm? Undoubtedly the union underwent many setbacks, not least continued membership decline, which by 2000 had fallen to 858,000. But this was also a period of necessary readjustment, with some positive gains, notably for women and black members. The TGWU, in common with the TUC and many other unions, made major modifications to its own structures and organising templates in this period. This was in addition to changes in negotiating procedures and priorities – some of which emanated from the new social partnership mantra and some of which were necessitated by the managerialist offensive aimed at jettisoning collective bargaining altogether. However, at the same time, internal disputes flared up within the TGWU and these had to be resolved at the same time as the union struggled to readjust its outward-facing policies and practices. The underlying political character of these disputes was masked by their seemingly organisational appearance: in other words, the form these internal wrangles took belied their sharp left/right political content.

Internal Problems

The election of Ron Todd as TGWU general secretary in 1985 ushered in a divisive period in the internal affairs of the union. The general secretary election was held in 1984, and although Todd topped the poll with a 45,000 lead over his nearest rival, George Wright, Todd did not take office until the following year. This was because of accusations of 'ballot rigging', and despite the fact that the outgoing general secretary (Moss Evans) rejected the charge, Todd insisted, in an undated handwritten letter to Evans, that a fresh election be held, 'not because of press pressure but for [the] good reputation of the union'.[13] Accordingly, a repeat ballot was held in 1985. This resulted in Todd's victory over Wright, who was the only other candidate. However, Todd's convincing victory in the second ballot did little to curtail internal strife within the TGWU. During his period of office the union was embroiled in a struggle between the (broad) left and right factions, which to some extent mirrored similar divisions within the Labour Party at the time. Len McCluskey was central to the formation of the national 'broad left' in the TGWU. Although the union had always been considered as a left-wing union, there was no organised left network until the 1980s. McCluskey recounts in his memoirs that he was given time off in the early 1980s

---

13 Ron Todd Archive, MRC MSS.572/36. Election of Ron Todd, 'ballot rigging'.

from his full-time official post (as secretary of the Association of Clerical, Technical and Supervisory Staff (ACTSS), the white-collar section of the TGWU), to 'become the secretariat' of the new broad left – an organisation which he described as 'shambolic but effective'.[14]

Although he was the candidate of the broad left, Todd sought, albeit unsuccessfully, to build unity with the right. However, disunity was clearly apparent in subsequent elections to the GEC, none more so than the GEC elections of 1990 – the first to be conducted by postal ballot. In this election, once again, the charge of ballot rigging was raised, provoking malevolent media interest. Todd was so concerned by the damage to the union's reputation and the resultant public furore that he kept a detailed handwritten record in diary form, covering, in three thick notebooks, every detail of all meetings, correspondence and personal conversations he had during the course of events leading up to the allegations, the subsequent inquiry and the ensuing re-ballot.[15]

In February 1990, Todd received a phone call from Owen Thomas of the Electoral Reform Society (ERC) saying that he had identified a 'major fraud in the elections'.[16] He reported a 'sudden surge of returned ballot papers' with identical crosses. These ballot papers – 9,580 in total – all came from Transport House (TGWU headquarters). Todd reacted swiftly. He wrote: 'It was obvious that what we were looking at was a conspiracy to defraud an election.' Thus he decided that the entire election should be re-run, even though he had been urged by 'the moderates' (Todd's terminology) that it was only necessary to re-ballot the fraudulent returns, which they deemed had come from broad left supporters. Needless to say, the press had a field day and were quick to castigate the left as the miscreants. Andrew Grice, a journalist from *The Times*, commented on the wider political significance of the election, which, he said, 'is vital to Neil Kinnock's hopes of presenting a moderate Labour image in the run up to the next general election'.[17] A second ballot was held after the resignation of the independent scrutineer, Rhys Vaughan, who was forced out after a vicious media attack impugning his honesty. The fact that the second ballot resulted in a five-seat majority for the left on the GEC (22:17) did little to resolve the political tension in the union. It was a pyrrhic victory.

The left/right division within the union was plainly apparent well before 1990. Todd himself had noted in 1988 the 'internal intrigue' in the TGWU. He observed that 'currently there is a new dimension which is disastrous for the union [...] the so called "new realism" – the two

14 Len McCluskey, *Always Red* (OR Books, 2021), p.44.

15 Ron Todd Archive, MRC MSS.572/28 and MSS.572/29.

16 All quotes are from Ron Todd's handwritten diaries, Ron Todd Archive, MRC MSS.572/28 and MSS.572/29.

17 Grice's article, 'Left Accused of Rigging Key T&G Election', is pasted in to one of Todd's diaries. Ron Todd Archive, MRC MSS.572/28 and MSS.572/29.

camp syndrome is always there – it is manifest in every election and every appointment'.[18] The 'two camp syndrome' was the broad left and the organised right. Todd cited as evidence the election of Brian Nicholson as chair of the GEC, replacing the left-winger Walter Greendale. It is now known that Nicholson had a close association with MI5. Whether or not he was an agent is unclear, but it is certain that he passed information to the Secret Service during the dock strikes in the 1970s in the period of the Heath government. Perhaps even more serious was Nicholson's divisive right-wing role in the TGWU and its wider political implications. For this he was lauded by the right-wing press, especially the *Daily Mail*, as Richard Littlejohn's panegyric following Nicholson's death clearly indicates:

> Brian was pivotal to Labour's revival, capturing control of the TGWU and using its mighty block vote to rout the hard Left and support the adoption of more moderate policies reasonable people could actually vote for. It may be an exaggeration to say that without Brian Nicholson, Tony Blair couldn't have become leader and eventually Prime Minister. But Brian and others prepared the ground, put in the hard yards – often in the teeth of fierce hostility from former comrades.[19]

In relation to non-elected posts, Todd cited examples of the appointment of two full-time regional officials in which a left incumbent or candidate was replaced by a right-wing nemesis. In Region 7, the Scottish regional secretary Hugh Wyper was succeeded by Dave Stoat, and in Region 1 (London and SE), Sid Staden was succeeded as regional secretary by Ken Reid. This is despite the fact that members in both regions supported alternative left-leaning candidates, notably Willy Queen in Scotland and Barry Camfield in Region 1. However, the appointment of regional local officers – district officers, district secretaries, regional trade group secretaries, regional education officers, etc. – was not (and still is not) the purview of the members or of their elected committees. For their appointment a panel of three GEC members was convened (known as the Examining Committee) to make the appointment; their decision would be ratified at the next meeting of the Finance and General Purposes Committee. The politicking would be to get the majority of the Examining Committee of the 'correct' political persuasion. For the appointment of senior officers, regional secretaries, national officers/secretaries and above, the full GEC was the interview panel.

---

18 Ron Todd Archive, MRC MSS.572/28 and MSS.572/29.
19 Richard Littlejohn, 'Patriotic, Moderate Labour Is Dead and Buried', *Daily Mail*, 22 February 2018. www.dailymail.co.uk/debate/article-5424497/Patriotic-moderate-Labour-dead-buried.html.

Docks

Two major industrial defeats added to the TGWU's problems in the Todd years. The most significant was the abolition of the National Dock Labour Scheme (NDLS), in 1989. The NDLS was established in 1946 by the Dock Workers (Regulation of Employment) Act. It gave security to RDWs who worked in NDLS ports. The scheme was intended to end the scourge of casual labour by giving dockers the legal right to minimum work, holidays, sick pay and pensions. It established a National Dock Labour Board consisting of 50 per cent union and 50 per cent employer representatives. But, as we have seen, the scheme was unpopular with the government and was detested by the port employers, who constantly sought to undermine it. In fact, by 1989, only 40 out of 75 British ports were covered by the NDLS, employing a total of 9,400 RDWs, more than 5,000 fewer than in 1983. Abolition of the scheme was a long-standing aim of the National Association of Port Employers (NAPE), as its director, Nicholas Finney, candidly revealed:

> Getting rid of the restrictions on the waterfront meant a whole new world in 'investment opportunity'. We sought two benefits from this approach. One, to make it much more difficult for the Labour Party and for the unions to argue against repeal, and secondly to make sure we could drive a wedge home to isolate dockers and describe them as a selfish, small group of workers who were actually stopping people from gaining jobs in unemployment blackspots which frequently were in under-developed city dock areas which had been derelict for many years.[20]

The government concurred. The Employment Secretary, Norman Fowler, told MPs that the NDLS had become 'a total anachronism' which stood in the way of a modern and efficient ports industry, and thus it was abolished by parliament in 1989.

Following abolition, the TGWU sought to minimise the damage by retaining national collective bargaining. This demand was rejected by the port employers, who were determined, as NAPE director Finney boasted later, to remove all national and local port agreements and to introduce 'new industrial contracts based entirely on the relationship with each employer's own workforce'.[21]

In response, John Connolly, secretary of the TGWU's historically powerful Docks and Waterways Group, called a delegate conference of

20 This is an extract from a speech delivered in Australia in 1990 by Nicholas Finney, 'Thatcherite Plan to Destroy National Dock Labour Scheme'. www.labournet.net/docks2/9706/NDLS.HTM.

21 Finney, 'Thatcherite Plan to Destroy National Dock Labour Scheme'.

dock workers which voted by 85 votes to 10 in favour of strike action. This action was confirmed by an overwhelming majority in a ballot of the RDWs in favour of strike action on a 90 per cent turnout. The battle lines were drawn, but a protracted legal battle ensued, initiated by NAPE, resulting in an injunction to prevent the strike. Having lost its case in the Court of Appeal, the TGWU successfully appealed to the House of Lords and a second ballot was held, leading to a strike of 96 per cent of RDWs. However, the government ensured that Royal Assent was given to the abolition of the NDLS *before* the appeal to the Lords. The NDLS no longer existed, and so the striking dockers were 'denied the Scheme's protection against dismissals, and the employers' success was virtually assured'.[22] NAPE now issued compulsory redundancy notices, resulting, as intended, in mass dismissals and a consequent weakening of the strike such that it was called off, on 1 August 1989. Over 2,000 dockers were either dismissed or threatened with dismissal during the strike.[23] At the end of the strike, the dock workforce had been halved. Casual labour replaced dismissed dockers. Of particular concern was the dismissal in July 1989 of 19 shop stewards employed by the Port of London Authority (PLA) at the Tilbury container port. Tilbury remained the only port on strike. The TGWU demanded the reinstatement of the sacked stewards, but in the face of PLA intransigence, and an unsuccessful Industrial Tribunal (IT) ruling, Todd asked the future Labour leader, Tony Blair, to raise questions in parliament.[24] The case dragged on 'through the longest Industrial Tribunal in British history'.[25] Ultimately, in August 1990, a subsequent IT ruled that 12 of the stewards had been wrongfully dismissed and ordered their reinstatement.[26] The remaining seven men received financial compensation.[27]

Such was the ignominious end to the heroic struggles of the TGWU and its predecessor unions to end the deprivation, poverty, appalling working conditions and insecure employment of British dock workers. The traditional militancy of dockers had secured major improvements, from the famous 1889 Great Dock Strike (and many others) to the 1920 Shaw Inquiry (and many others) to the zenith of the establishment of the NDLS. Its abolition in 1989, ironically, or perhaps significantly, marked the

22 Roy Mankelow, 'The Effects of the 1980s Employment Legislation in Britain on the Protection of Workers' Rights: The Case of the London Dock-Workers', *International Contributions to Labour Studies*, 1996, vol.6, p.133. https://cpes.org.uk/om/files/original/5aeda81de7f29999c3707f092611f7b6.pdf.

23 Peter Southwood, *British Dockers: A Survey of Human Rights in the Former Scheme Ports* (Transport and General Workers' Union, 1992).

24 Ron Todd Archive, MRC MSS.572/42. Letter to Tony Blair, 20 June 1990.

25 Mankelow, 'The Effects of the 1980s Employment Legislation', p.138.

26 This did not materialise.

27 *Port of London Authority* v. *Payne & Others* [1993] EWCA Civ J1103-8, 3 November 1993. https://vlex.co.uk/vid/port-of-london-authority-793660781.

centenary of the Great Dock Strike. All was now in ruins and the union was broken – a nadir for the TGWU, a crowing victory for the rapacious port employers backed by the Tory government. Nicholas Finney boasted that:

- We removed all port agreements, seventy in all.
- We removed all industry Conciliation and Arbitration procedures.
- We introduced new industrial contracts based entirely on the relationship with each employer's own workforce.
- We developed entirely new work patterns, totally flexible shift patterns.
- We eliminated labour pooling.
- We introduced part time working/contracting out.

[...]

> But I think the greatest of our achievements (and this is an achieve-ment for the company as a whole) is that we destroyed for the foreseeable future the power of trade unions to hold the country to ransom by calling a national dock strike, which is so wrong for any democratically elected government.[28]

Len McCluskey shared Jack Jones's view that, given the long-standing threat to the NDLS, the union should have developed an alternative strategy to withstand the inevitable attack. Jones was even more critical of what he regarded as the union's 'constitutional approach'. He wrote:

> The spirit was hounded out of us by Thatcherism, quite deliber-ately so. And we reacted in a rather constitutional way. [...] when the National Dock Labour Scheme was abolished it should have been challenged straightaway by strike action.[29]

Ford Dundee

The Docks defeat followed another pivotal defeat for the TGWU three years earlier, in 1987. This centred on the employers seeking to exploit political divisions within the trade union movement, which in practice meant that they would offer trade union recognition (as in the case of Wapping) to the least-militant trade union. In this case, Ford EED

28 Extract from Finney, 'Thatcherite Plan to Destroy National Dock Labour Scheme'. These are a selection from his bullet-pointed list.
29 Quoted in Andrew Murray, *The T&G Story: A History of the Transport and General Workers Union, 1922–2007* (Lawrence & Wishart, 2008), p.185.

(Electronics and Engineering Division) proposed to establish a new factory in Dundee on the basis of a single-union agreement with their union of choice – the Amalgamated Engineering Union (AEU). Well aware of the strategic similarity with the EEPTU's single-union deal at Wapping (see Chapter 6), the TGWU and other unions with an interest in the Dundee plant referred the matter to the TUC. TUC representatives then travelled to Ford headquarters in Detroit in order to negotiate an acceptable agreement. This mission failed, with the consequence that Ford withdrew its proposal to open a new plant in Dundee. Following Ford's withdrawal, the general secretary of the AEU, Gavin Laird, together with Malcolm Rifkind (Secretary of State for Scotland), attacked the TGWU for losing the Ford contract and the jobs that went with it. Ken Gill, general secretary of the newly formed Manufacturing, Science and Finance union (MSF), castigated what he saw as the unholy alliance between a trade union and the Tory government. Gill wrote, 'when Tory ministers and a trade union leader unite, trade unionists are entitled to smell a rat'.[30] He was right to smell a rat – Laird went ahead and negotiated a single-union deal with Ford behind everyone's back, and the Dundee plant opened on that basis – AEU only. The TGWU maintained its opposition, saying its objection was not just due to the single-union agreement but to the fact that the wages in the Dundee plant were lower than in other Ford plants, in breach of nationally negotiated agreements. Interestingly enough, as the letter in Figure 13 shows, on the basis of a resolution proposed, significantly, by two members of the AEU, the Ford Shop Stewards' Committee confirmed the TGWU's objection to the Dundee deal.[31]

The TGWU Scottish regional secretary, David Shoat, complained about media coverage of the issue. He pointed out that despite the fact that ten unions objected to the terms Ford EED was seeking to impose, the press singled out only one union for censure – the TGWU. Shoat's statement made a further important point of clarification in relation to the substantive issue: 'the argument is not about a single-union agreement, or about which union will have the membership, but the potential undermining of the Ford UK national agreement'.[32]

In the light of the Ford Dundee debacle, the BDC in 1989 debated the issue of 'sweetheart deals'. Delegates gave ample evidence of the preponderance of such deals in other industries and expressed anger at the failure of the TUC to enforce the Bridlington Agreement, which dealt with relations between unions and the settlement of disputes. It was pointed

30 Ron Todd Archive, MRC MSS.572/57. See Ken Gill, 'A Test of Trade Union Validity in the Face of Corporate Arrogance', *Independent*, 31 March 1988.
31 Ron Todd Archive, MRC MSS.572/57.
32 Statement on Dundee from TGWU Scottish Region, 24 March 1988. Ron Todd Archive, MRC MSS.572/57.

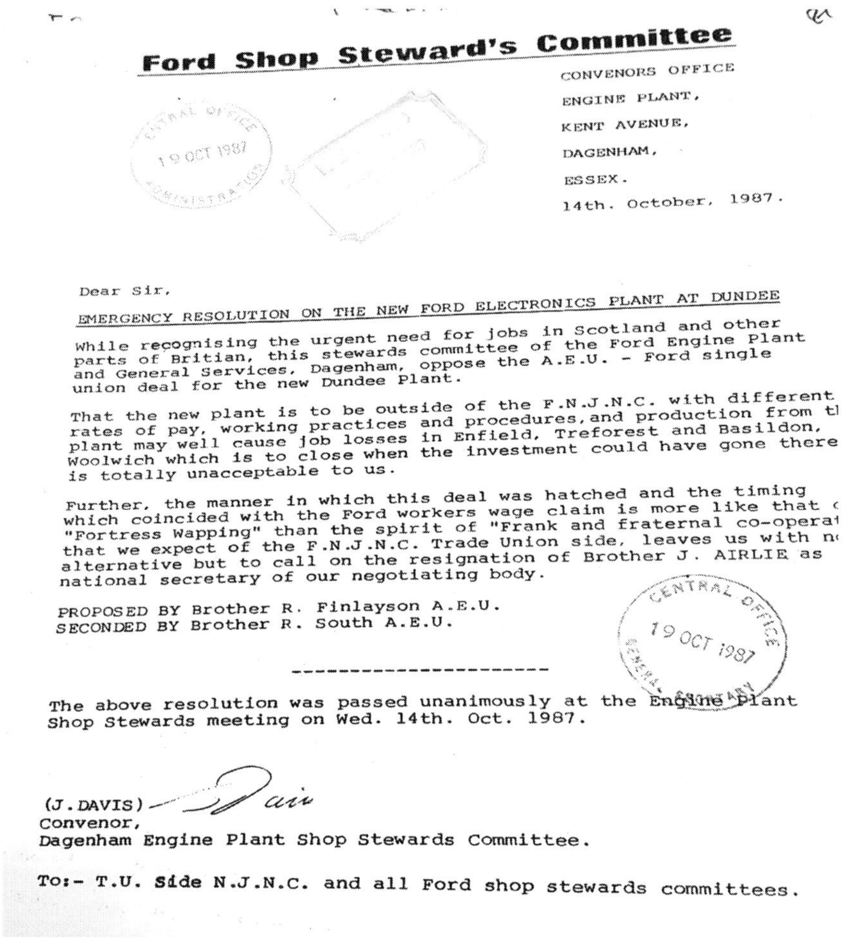

Ford Shop Steward's Committee

CONVENORS OFFICE
ENGINE PLANT,
KENT AVENUE,
DAGENHAM,
ESSEX.
14th. October, 1987.

CENTRAL OFFICE 19 OCT 1987 ADMINISTRATION

Dear Sir,

EMERGENCY RESOLUTION ON THE NEW FORD ELECTRONICS PLANT AT DUNDEE

While recognising the urgent need for jobs in Scotland and other parts of Britian, this stewards committee of the Ford Engine Plant and General Services, Dagenham, oppose the A.E.U. - Ford single union deal for the new Dundee Plant.

That the new plant is to be outside of the F.N.J.N.C. with different rates of pay, working practices and procedures, and production from th plant may well cause job losses in Enfield, Treforest and Basildon, Woolwich which is to close when the investment could have gone there is totally unacceptable to us.

Further, the manner in which this deal was hatched and the timing which coincided with the Ford workers wage claim is more like that o "Fortress Wapping" than the spirit of "Frank and fraternal co-operat that we expect of the F.N.J.N.C. Trade Union side, leaves us with no alternative but to call on the resignation of Brother J. AIRLIE as national secretary of our negotiating body.

PROPOSED BY Brother R. Finlayson A.E.U.
SECONDED BY Brother R. South A.E.U.

CENTRAL OFFICE 19 OCT 1987 GENERAL SECRETARY

The above resolution was passed unanimously at the Engine Plant Shop Stewards meeting on Wed. 14th. Oct. 1987.

(J.DAVIS) Davis
Convenor,
Dagenham Engine Plant Shop Stewards Committee.

To:- T.U. Side N.J.N.C. and all Ford shop stewards committees.

Figure 13: Emergency resolution of the new Ford electronics plant at Dundee

out that 1989 marked the 50th anniversary of the Bridlington Agreement. Such was the anger that the GEC was instructed

> to examine the terms and operation of the Bridlington Agreement to establish whether it serves the best interests of this union and consider our relationship with the TUC in the context of what is most beneficial to the interests of trade unionism in general and the TGWU in particular.[33]

33 Verbatim minutes, 1989 TGWU BDC, composite motion 43, Unite archive, Holborn.

Internationalism and South Africa

Ron Todd was Chair of the TUC International Committee. He visited South Africa on a trade union mission in 1986 and was a strong supporter of the Anti-Apartheid Movement and the independent trade union lobby in South Africa. In an extensive interview with Christabel Gurney, Todd explained that his commitment to internationalism led to his early involvement in the Anti-Apartheid Movement well before it became a major trade union issue.[34] He recalled that when he spoke at an anti-apartheid fringe meeting at the 1978 TUC congress, he 'got in trouble over it' on the spurious grounds that he supported violence in South Africa, to which he replied 'violence had been going on for three decades'.

Before he became TGWU general secretary, Todd had been a shop steward and deputy convenor at Ford Dagenham. While there, he initiated practical trade union solidarity with striking workers at the Ford plant in Port Elizabeth in South Africa. The TGWU members at Ford UK needed little persuasion to support fellow trade unionists in South Africa whose picket lines were being subjected to police violence. So, in Todd's words,

> We told the Ford Motor Company of our intentions, 'You either talk to your South African partners in Ford in Port Elizabeth and you either tell them to pull back from what they're doing or we will stop all KD [knock-down components] from going from Dagenham to Port Elizabeth', and Ford's said, 'We can't interfere with the South African government'. We said, 'All right then, no KD. We are not sending any packets out to South Africa.' Within a few days we found it had all changed – they were recognising the strikers. [...] There was tremendous pressure from the Ford workers, from the 24 plants, there was pressure within the company.[35]

Todd acknowledged that he was following in the footsteps of Moss Evans, who also had been Chairman of the International Committee of the TUC. Evans had very forcefully indicated that the TGWU would give total support in the fight against apartheid – morally, physically and financially. Thus, when Todd became general secretary, it was clear that he was taking up the Evans mantle and that his internationalist views were well known. In his view, this explained why he had GEC support in continuing vigorously to oppose the apartheid regime (Figure 14). This

---

34 Interview with Ron Todd, 22 March 2004, reproduced in the Anti-Apartheid Movement archives. www.aamarchives.org/archive/interviews/ron-todd/int09t-ron-todd-transcript.html.

35 Interview with Ron Todd, 22 March 2004, p.2

Figure 14:
'United Against Racism'
(T&G Record, Unite
the Union)

support was unwavering to the extent that he took pride in the fact that the GEC 'supported my call when, on a number of occasions, I said if our government would not impose sanctions against South Africa, the T&G would support any group of workers who took action against apartheid'.[36]

Unilateralism

For the TGWU, and for the entire labour movement, the 1980s was a decade of defeat. This decade coincided with Ron Todd's period of office, a period in which the right had triumphed and it appeared that the 'forward march' of labour had indeed been halted. However, the battle continued and, in policy terms at least, Todd personally can be credited with a significant victory. In 1989, the BDC held a debate on the issue of the TGWU's long-standing support for British unilateral nuclear disarmament – a policy no longer supported by the Labour Party. A composite motion opposing unilateralism argued that this policy on nuclear weapons would impede the prospect of returning a Labour government.[37] It went on

36 Interview with Ron Todd, 22 March 2004, p.1.
37 Verbatim minutes, 1989 TGWU BDC, motion 28, Unite archive, Holborn.

to call for a secret postal ballot of the entire membership, to be held before the 1990 Labour Party conference, on the choice between multilateralism and unilateralism. This was Todd's last congress and he used it to make a moving and impassioned speech in support of TGWU policy on nuclear weapons. He said:

> For thirty years this great union has kept up its clear and logical stand on the futility and barbarity of nuclear weapons. As a shop steward at Ford's I marched with many of you here behind the proud banner of CND. We pursued it under Frank Cousins, under Jack Jones and under Moss Evans. It is the single policy that has given me most pride as a member of the Transport and General Workers Union. It is a policy which, as General Secretary, I felt the most honour in defending. It is a policy we celebrate every year when we give the Frank Cousins Peace Award. [...] Don't abandon it now colleagues. Don't fudge the truth, not for anyone's convenience.[38]

Todd was given a standing ovation: motion 28 was defeated and the TGWU's long-standing policy of British unilateral nuclear disarmament was maintained.

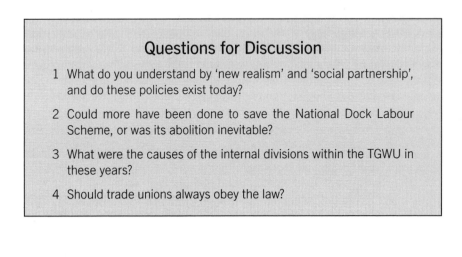

Questions for Discussion

1 What do you understand by 'new realism' and 'social partnership', and do these policies exist today?

2 Could more have been done to save the National Dock Labour Scheme, or was its abolition inevitable?

3 What were the causes of the internal divisions within the TGWU in these years?

4 Should trade unions always obey the law?

---

38 Todd's reply, verbatim minutes, 1989 TGWU BDC.

7

Equalities: Women Members, Black Members

Pressure on trade unions to reverse their historical neglect of women and black members came from three sources. The first, and most important, was from the members themselves. The second impetus came from the necessity in the face of anti-union laws and declining membership to recruit more members from beyond the traditional white male demographic. The third source of pressure was to be found in the growth and influence of organisations outside the labour movement, notably the Women's Liberation Movement and the Black Liberation Movement. Additionally, the Gay Liberation Movement also impacted on unions' increased awareness of discriminatory practices. The dawning consciousness that equality issues had hitherto been neglected in word and deed led to the beginnings of policy changes in this period. The impact of these movements among oppressed and discriminated swathes of the population served as a reminder that the basic principle of trade unionism, summed up in the slogan 'an injury to one is an injury to all', had been honoured hitherto only in the breach.

Women

The whole post-war era is remarkable for the relentless rise of paid female employment, so that, by 2000, women constituted half of the employed labour force. Trade unions were slow to recognise this fact, but change was inevitable whether it was motivated by conviction or survival. Progress, however, was slow, and even slower in unions like the TGWU, which had a small percentage of women members.

However, in 2000, 38.5 per cent of the affiliated membership to the TUC was female. Women numerically dominated many large public service unions, with 92 per cent of members in the Royal College of Nursing (RCN), 72 per cent in UNISON, 59 per cent in the Public and Commercial Services Union (PCS) and, in the two largest schoolteachers' unions, 76 per cent in the National Union of Teachers (NUT) and 60 per cent in the National Association of Schoolmasters Union of Women Teachers (NASUWT). This was not generally translated into leading positions, as a survey of 62 unions in 1992 found less than 12 per cent of full-time officers to be women, and in that year only 24 per cent of TUC delegates were women.

In 1979, TGWU BDC adopted a 'comprehensive' policy on women (Figure 15). It mainly covered issues relating to 'the special problems faced by women workers and female trade unionists'.[1] In attempting to offer remedies, the motion was particularly concerned by 'the lack of confidence of many women at union meeting and conferences'. At the time there were roughly 350,000 women members of the TGWU – 16.4 per cent of the total. However, as the *Women's Handbook* admitted, there were no women on the union's 'elected constitutional committees or amongst the full-time officials'.[2]

Closely influenced by the 1979 TUC Charter on Equality for Women in Trade Unions, the TGWU policy offered positive steps to encourage women's participation in the affairs of the union. Such measures included the provision of crèche facilities at meetings and conferences outside working hours, education courses for women, and the establishment of women's committees, regionally or nationally, 'to investigate these problems and to encourage women's participation'. Some progress was made on this, but clearly it was insufficient, as a (defeated) BDC motion some years later (1989) pointed out. It said that existing facilities at summer schools were 'a deterrent for any person to attend' and went on to suggest that the major cause of the small numbers of women participants at all levels of the union was 'inadequate child care facilities'.[3]

The 1989 BDC, recognising that women now constituted almost 50 per cent of the British workforce, adopted a far-reaching policy on women in employment and called for 'a concerted campaign of collective bargaining on the following issues: child care, women returners, hours of work, training for women, women's health, paternity leave, career breaks, women's pay'.[4] The 1989 BDC is noteworthy because, according to National Advisory Committee officer Margaret Prosser, it was 'the best debate on equal opportunities for a long time', possibly because it addressed other equality issues. For the first time, a motion on lesbian and gay rights for the repeal of Section 28 (the series of laws introduced by the Thatcher government that prohibited the 'promotion of homosexuality' by local authorities) was passed (although there was some opposition to

1 *Women's Handbook: Policies and Action for the Transport and General Workers' Union* (TGWU, 1980).

2 *Women's Handbook*, p.32.

3 Verbatim minutes, 1989 TGWU BDC, Unite archive, Holborn.

4 Verbatim minutes, 1989 TGWU BDC.

Figure 15: Cover of *Women's*
Handbook (TGWU, 1980)

this). A policy on disability rights was also adopted. A motion on abortion was more controversial. It reaffirmed the TGWU's pro-choice policy and support for the National Abortion Campaign, including extending abortion services to Northern Ireland.

A National Women's Advisory Committee (NWAC) was established in October 1984, chaired by Jane McKay. Following the appointment of Yvonne Strachan as Scottish Women's Organiser in 1985, most regions followed suit and duly sent women's representatives to sit on the NWAC. It is clear, however, that not all Regional Women's Advisory Committees functioned smoothly, as the observations below from Val Burn, a woman activist from North East, Yorkshire and Humberside Region, indicate.

In 1988, the first issue of a quarterly TGWU's women's magazine was published, named *T&G Women* (later renamed *Together* as the bulletin of the NWAC). This, and each subsequent issue, gave examples of the work of Regional Women's Advisory Committees, with a spotlight on individual regions in turn. When Diana Holland was appointed as Region 1 women's officer in 1990, she discovered that she was one of only 3 per cent of women full-time officials.[5] Unsurprisingly, she also found that the two most

---

5 Interview with Diana Holland, Unite archive, Holborn.

Women's Advisory Committees of the TGWU, Established in 1985

Val Burn

(North East, Yorkshire and Humberside Region)

Yes, Only 'Advisory'

As a woman within the Region, the first awareness re the Advisory Committee was that, as an active Woman rep, you were invited to become a member of the Regional Advisory Committee by your Officer.

As the Humber area was the old Region 10, the Regional office was in Hull, so all meetings of the then Region 10 were held in the Hull office quarterly.

At this time the present Unite Region was as follows:

Humberside	Region 10
Leeds Area	Region 9
Newcastle Area	Region 8

In Region 10, there were eight women on the Regional Women's Committee. At first, you were invited to submit your items to the regional secretary for the Agenda. If we raised anything, we were quickly reminded that we were 'advisory', and if anything was discussed and we wanted to achieve it, it would have to be put on the agenda for the Regional Committee to discuss it, and then it would be fed back to us. We quickly realised what 'advisory' meant – no teeth – not in the rule book – purely 'advisory'.

Each Regional Women's Committee had to elect a delegate to the National Women's Committee. The National Advisory Committee officer was the national officer, Margaret Prosser.

At the National Women's Advisory Committee, when trying to make progress for women to become further involved, we were always reminded that we were 'advisory' only. Frustration became the name of the game and so we set about how to take our rightful place in the union.

We submitted a motion to the Policy Conference, and women went back to their branches and got themselves elected to the Policy Conference to support the motion. Once there, we were then told it was a Rules Conference issue – so we had to wait for the next Rules Conference, which, at that time, it was every six years.

Hey ho. We then went to the next Rules Conference and went before the standing orders committee. And, sadly to say, it was all men on the committee. Whereupon we were told it could not go on the agenda and therefore it would have to go back to the Policy Conference. When asked the question why, the chair replied it was a policy business. We were certainly given a bum steer. Thus it was not on the agenda for the Rules Conference, so it was not discussed.

If you check back you will see it was in the 1990s (approx. 9 years) before we became a Committee within the rule book, and we then took our rightful place in the TGWU. If you also check back you will see that the National Race Advisory and the Disability Advisory Committees also took their rightful place in the rule book some months later, after the women had taken their place. The National Women's Committee was thanked for their hard work and determination for leading the way, which had also helped the other two National Committees, who too had similar stories to share.

This also led to a representative from those committees to take a place on the General Executive Committee.

common problems experienced by women members – pregnancy discrimination and sexual harassment – had been systematically ignored by male officers. The appointment of regional women's officers changed this culture and paved the way for more women to want to be involved in the union, as it gradually came to be seen as representing their needs as workers and as trade unionists. In answer to a question raised at the 1989 BDC on the number of women full-time officers, Margaret Prosser replied that there were 18 out of 500, and that this represented 3 per cent, whereas women's membership of the union stood at 18 per cent. Clearly, she said, this was not proportionate 'and nowhere as good as we would like it to be. However, it is an improvement compared with what we saw a few years ago.'[6]

The TUC 'Charter for Equality' was revised in 1990. It recommended key targets for women's participation and advocated 'proportionality' in terms of women's involvement in unions' decision-making structures. This was a goal which the TGWU was already pursuing.

In 1990, the National Women's Advisory Committee published a five-year plan entitled 'Strategy for Women and Equality'.[7] It covered the following seven key overarching priorities by which progress should be monitored:

1 Organising, recruiting and servicing women members;

2 Mainstreaming women's equality in all TGWU sectors and regions;

3 Bargaining for women: industrial strategies and workplace monitoring;

6 Margaret Prosser, verbatim minutes, 1989 TGWU BDC, Unite archive, Holborn.
7 MRC MSS.1086/2/74. T&G, 'Strategy for Women and Equality, 2000–2005'.

4 Improving education and communication for women's equality;

5 Campaigning against poverty, strengthening the welfare state and for simplified, strengthened sex equality law;

6 Extending links with women internationally and in Europe;

7 Building involvement of all women – black women, disabled women, young women, retired women and lesbians.

The 1993 BDC received the 'GEC Explanatory Statement on Equal Opportunities'. In introducing the statement, Margaret Prosser reviewed the progress the union had made on equalities. In a characteristically forthright assessment, she recounted the evolution of the union's equality policies since 1979. She argued that 'the development of equal opportunities within the union is not the same as trying to develop industrial policy'.[8] The latter went across all trade groups and all departments and as a result the development was patchy, although much good work had been accomplished in many sectors. This, she explained, was due to the difficulty of breaking through 'years of social attitudes, which put women in a particular place, [and] which did not recognise the qualities that black people can bring to our organisation', and that structural barriers persisted which failed to 'take account of everybody's different kinds of responsibilities'.[9]

In relation to women, Prosser accepted the criticism that in the last 18 months the union had not 'moved very energetically forward'. Despite this, she recounted the fact that 7 out of 8 regions now had regional women's officers and that other equality strands had been created, notably a disability forum and a lesbian and gay group. Several initiatives had also been established to remedy the under-representation of women and black members. Prompted by the requirement of the TUC and the Labour Party, the TGWU also now ensured that delegations to both these bodies reflected the proportion of women in the union. In addition, 'Changing the Face' had now been completed. This was a major TGWU consultation exercise, which although specifically established to look at the under-representation of women had resulted in a scheme of representation that ushered in the requirement for reserved seats for black and women members. Initiatives had also been taken, with the help of Ruskin College, to raise awareness of the requirement of equality in the employment practices of the TGWU as an employer. The implementation of such a policy and practice had been overseen by Prosser herself together with the regional women's officers and the race and women's advisory committees, which had, she reported, begun to draft a policy. She reminded the BDC that she had spent the last eight years of her working life developing equal

---

8 Verbatim minutes, 1993 TGWU BDC, Unite archive, Holborn.
9 Verbatim minutes, 1993 TGWU BDC.

Figure 16: 'Women like you ... join the T&G': 1990 recruitment leaflet
(TUC Library Collections)

opportunities policies for the union and latterly she had combined this with
her post as a national officer. She concluded by saying that 'I would not
be prepared to put this statement forward if I thought it was a mere sop'.

However, not all delegates shared Margaret Prosser's optimistic
portrayal of the progress of equal opportunities in the union. Sister
Burn, from Region 10, said that the statement was a disappointment
and that it merely constituted a documentation of what was already in
existence. She compared the TGWU's policy unfavourably with that

of UNISON. Another delegate (Sister Fernandez, Region 6) expressed serious concern with the executive statement. She pointed out that despite the fact that a TGWU conference had been held to raise awareness of equal opportunities for the GEC, it had attracted less than 50 per cent of the members of this committee, and of those in attendance most were there only part of the time. She was highly critical of the TGWU as an employer and in particular of the fact that each region had a different recruitment and selection procedure. The statement proclaimed that most regions have ensured that their full-time officers have attended race awareness training; however, she asserted that there was no evidence that this had actually taken place. She also compared the TGWU with UNISON and stated that the latter had an equal opportunities strategy which was attracting large numbers of women to membership (Figure 16).

Whatever the difficulties, it was undeniable that, after a history of nigh-on exclusion, women were at last being seen and heard in the TGWU. Progress had been slow and painstaking, but by 1990, national and regional women's committees were up and running, policies for women were advanced and at last the hitherto all-male bastion of the GEC had been pierced by three women: Maureen Twomey, Carol Rowe and Margaret Cassidy.

Education Courses for Women

Seen as 'a breakthrough for women in the union',[10] the TGWU held its first women's educational course in 1980. The main tutor was a man – Pete Batten. Nonetheless, a regular series of women's courses followed in which women tutors and educators played an increasingly prominent role. When, in 1985, Margaret Prosser's national officer post was upgraded to National Secretary for Women, swift progress was made not only on trade union education for women, regionally and nationally, but also on all the other aspects of 'positive discrimination' adopted in 1979 and reaffirmed at the BDCs in 1983 and 1989.

By 1990, according to John Fisher,

> Women's education had become an established part of the union's programme, and by the third quarter of 1990 the number of women members on courses was brought to an approximate *pro rata* position of 20% of the total.[11]

---

10 John Fisher, *Bread on the Waters: A History of TGWU Education 1922–2000* (Lawrence & Wishart, 2005).
11 Fisher, *Bread on the Waters*, p.239.

Education by and for women members together with the appointment of Regional Women's Organisers (RWOs) had an important impact on women's involvement in the union. After becoming the first woman to be appointed as a national officer, Margaret Prosser, in an interview, said that the education programme of the union was one of the most important ways of overcoming the obstacles that prevent women from becoming more active.[12]

Black Workers and Race

The 1970s were characterised by a 'colour-blind' approach to black workers on the part of most trade unions. This was exemplified by a statement in 1970 by the TUC general secretary, Vic Feather, that 'the trade union movement is concerned with a man or woman as a worker. The colour of a man's skin has no relevance whatever to his work.'[13] The TUC and some individual unions started to develop educational and training materials on equal opportunities, and in 1979 the TUC called on its affiliates to adopt a policy on racism. However, in these early days, action against racism and race discrimination was still notable by its absence. In 1974, a House of Commons Select Committee complained that

> the record of the TUC is similar to that of the CBI [*the employers' organisation*] in that both organisations have declared their opposition to racial discrimination, but have taken wholly inadequate steps to ensure that their members work effectively to eradicate it.[14]

As trade unions came under attack in 1979 during the Thatcher era, and as membership levels began to decline sharply, it was increasingly clear that black workers, who formed one of the most loyal sections of the membership of most trade unions, including the TGWU, could no longer be ignored. From the black workers' point of view, however, it also became increasingly clear that there was little appetite among many in the white trade union leadership to deal with the racism that black workers faced from their white workmates – often fellow trade union members – or from the employer. This led black workers to fall back on what they knew from their history of resisting slavery and colonialism – that collectively organising as black workers could bring results.

12 MRC MSS.126/TG/1379/A/28/1. *Together*, 1992/3, vol.3.
13 Quoted in John Wrench, 'Unequal Comrades: Trade Unions, Equal Opportunity and Racism', University of Warwick, Policy Papers in Ethnic Relations No.5, 1986, p.8. https://warwick.ac.uk/fac/soc/crer/research/publications/policy/policyp_no.5.pdf.
14 Quoted by Wrench, 'Unequal Comrades', p.11.

Informal meetings of black workers in many unions – particularly in the public services – started to take place. The aim was to provide solidarity, to share information on their plight and to begin to map out a strategy for exerting more influence within their trade unions. Inevitably, this strategy always appeared to have two key planks. First, that the union should recognise the right of black workers to self-organise within its formal structures, and second, that resources should be made available to support this process.

Some unions, after having initially refused to do so, did eventually agree to varying forms of black self-organisation in the early 1980s. The National and Local Government Officers' Association (NALGO – now part of UNISON), the National Union of Journalists (NUJ) and the National Association of Probation Officers (NAPO) all agreed to forms of black self-organisation.

During the same period, there was the development of unrecognised or informal black self-organised groups (often, at least initially, unrecognised by union leaderships) within other unions, such as the National Union of Public Employees (NUPE – now part of UNISON), the Confederation of Health Service Employees (COHSE – now part of UNISON), the Society of Civil and Public Servants (now part of the PCS) and the TGWU. The norm was for unions to establish advisory structures to their executive committees rather than providing the space for black self-organisation within their bodies. As Satnam Virdee notes, by the mid-1970s, 'there was a growing recognition amongst many white activists that racism in trade unions had to be tackled'.[15]

Much of this growth arose from the activities of the Black Trade Union Solidarity Movement and the later Labour Party Black Section-inspired Black Trade Union Forum. It was essentially the same people involved in these three bodies. They each contributed in their specific spheres of work to providing a cross-union approach to the development of black self-organisation. This allowed black activists to exchange intelligence on the strategies that were being pursued by trade union leaders either to resist the development of black self-organisation or to accommodate it within the formal structures of unions.[16] The inspiration for this long-awaited understanding was due, according to Virdee, to the activities of socialists and especially the Communist Party, which, he argues, helped to foster 'inter-racial class solidarity' of the kind seen at Grunwick.

In 1981, the TUC adopted its charter, 'Black Workers: A TUC Charter for Equality of Opportunity', calling on its affiliates to encourage

---

15 Satnam Virdee, 'A Marxist Critique of Black Radical Theories of Trade-Union Racism', *Sociology*, 2000, vol.34, no.3, pp.545–565.

16 Mary Davis, Roger McKenzie and Wilf Sullivan, *Working against Racism: The Role of Trade Unions in Britain* (Trades Union Congress, 2006).

greater participation of black and ethnic minority workers within their ranks through the creation of advisory committees, special education programmes and recruitment drives, and urging them to include discrimination issues in their collective bargaining agendas and to take vigorous action in defence of employment grievances involving racial harassment or discrimination

The issue of black participation in trade unions was initially raised within the TGWU in 1987. This conference passed a motion which, among other issues, condemned the racist propaganda of the press and called for 'a concerted campaign to eradicate racist attitudes' and 'for more assistance to ethnic minorities to achieve their full potential in the movement'.[17] Participants in the debate called upon the TGWU to put its own house in order and 'talk about eradicating some of the racist attitudes that still prevail in our union'.[18] The mover of the motion (Sister K. Crosby, Region 1) condemned the racist attitudes and practices of the government and the employers but declared that 'we should be starting here in this union, where we organise large numbers of black people and I say once again that it is actually disgraceful that there are so few black people here'.[19] Growing concern from the members on this issue led the 1987 BDC to decide that 'the union should set up a network of race advisory committees to promote the involvement of black and ethnic minority workers within the union'. This, in turn, led to the establishment in 1988 of an Equal Opportunities Working Party representing delegates from each of the union's 11 regions. It recommended that national and regional race advisory committees should be established and that a National Equal Opportunities Officer be appointed. These proposals were agreed by the TGWU GEC and endorsed by the 1989 BDC. Bob Purkiss was appointed as national officer in 1989, and the Race National and Regional Advisory Committees were established in 1990, with Carol Forfar as the national Chair. These committees would be responsible for advising on initiatives to promote the recruitment, organisation and involvement of minority ethnic members.[20] However, as acknowledged by the 1989 BDC, progress in establishing race advisory committees was slow 'because not all members are convinced of the need for race advisory committees'.[21] As Mohammad Taj explained,

---

17 Verbatim minutes, 1987 TGWU BDC, composite motion 14, Unite archive, Holborn.

18 Eric Rechnitz, verbatim minutes, 1987 TGWU BDC, composite motion 14.

19 Crosby, verbatim minutes, 1987 TGWU BDC, composite motion 14.

20 John Wrench and Satnam Virdee, 'Organising the Unorganised: "Race", Poor Work and Trade Unions', Project Report, Coventry Centre for Research in Ethnic Relations, University of Warwick, 1995.

21 Margaret Prosser's reply to the equal opportunities debate, verbatim minutes, 1989 TGWU BDC, Unite archive, Holborn.

I was one of those who voted at the 1987 BDC conference for change. There were close to 1,200 delegates but I'd guess there was not even ten delegates who were BAEM [Black, Asian Ethnic Minority]. Yet the TGWU had hundreds of thousands of BAEM members.[22]

In 1987, it was calculated that 23 per cent of trade union members from black, Asian ethnic minorities belonged to the TGWU.

A motion welcoming the Labour Party's commitment to repeal the 1971 and 1981 Immigration Acts was passed at the 1987 BDC. The motion also called for a 'concerted campaign to eradicate racist attitudes' and 'for more assistance to ethnic minorities to achieve their full potential in the movement'.[23] The motion was proposed by Sister K. Crosby. She condemned the escalation of police violence against black people but was also sharply critical of the TGWU's lack of assistance to its black members, saying that 'we unionise large numbers of black people [...] [but] it is actually disgraceful that there are so few black people here'.[24] This was echoed by the motion's seconder (Eric Rechnitz), who said that the union had to examine itself and 'eradicate some of the racist attitudes that still prevail'. Another delegate (I. Monckton, Region 4) warned that delegates should not think 'that you are not racists because you have passed composite 14'. Racism prevails in the union and 'the trouble is that a lot of people do not recognise it in themselves'.[25]

Education Courses for Black Members

John Fisher observes that in the 1980s race equality was given less prominence than women's equality, the assumption being that 'union members would not be racially prejudiced, and that the general message of worker solidarity would overcome xenophobic or racist feelings'.[26] This assumption was somewhat blemished by the experience of TGWU dockers marching in support of Enoch Powell in 1968. Although 'race issues' were included on many existing TGWU courses, it was not until the 1990s that race awareness courses and courses for black members got off the

---

22 Quoted in Mark Metcalf, *Mohammad Taj: Steering from the Front* (Unite, 2018), p.43. https://markwritecouk.files.wordpress.com/2018/09/6328dpmt2018-taj-booklet-web.pdf. Mohammad Taj was elected as TUC President in 2013. He was the first Asian and the first bus worker to hold the post of President.

23 Verbatim minutes, 1987 TGWU BDC, composite motion 14, Unite archive, Holborn.

24 Verbatim minutes, 1987 TGWU BDC, composite motion 14.

25 Verbatim minutes, 1987 TGWU BDC, composite motion 14.

26 Fisher, *Bread on the Waters*, p.239.

ground. The inclusion of equalities as a core subject, which all regions and the national programmes were mandatorily required to teach, led to the continuing presence of this subject in the education curriculum. The first black and ethnic members' weekend was conducted during the weekend of 1–3 June 1990, at Eastbourne. Twenty-three members attended, with three black lay tutors and Bob Purkiss.

Lesbian and Gay Members

It was not until 1991 that systematic attention was paid to discrimination faced by lesbian and gay members of the TGWU. Possibly in response to the government's attack on the gay community exemplified by section 28 of the Local Government Act, the union adopted a comprehensive policy on lesbian and gay rights at the 1991 BDC. Section 28 had been brought in on the back of the stigmatisation and discrimination suffered by gay men following the AIDS/HIV pandemic. Section 28 stated that a local authority shall not

(a) Intentionally promote homosexuality or publish material with the intention of promoting homosexuality;

(b) promote the teaching in any maintained school of the acceptability of homosexuality as a pretended family relationship.[27]

Composite motion 10 demanded the immediate repeal of section 28 and went on to affirm the union's commitment to 'the removal of all barriers and prejudice within the workplace in order that lesbian and gay men may have the same rights and security as other workers'.[28] It called for three policy changes:

To promote the inclusion of lesbian and gay rights within [negotiated] equal opportunities policies [...]

To review and amend the Union's services and benefits to ensure access by [same sex] partners [...]

To promote positive images of lesbian and gay men within the *Record* and other Union publications.[29]

27 Local Government Act 1988. www.legislation.gov.uk/ukpga/1988/9/section/28/enacted.
28 Verbatim minutes, 1991 TGWU BDC, Unite archive, Holborn.
29 Verbatim minutes, 1991 TGWU BDC.

Questions for Discussion

1 Why in your view did it take until the 1980s for the TGWU to recognise the existence of racism and sexism?

2 Why and how did attitudes change?

3 What more needs to be done?

8

Ireland: Working for Class Unity in Extreme Circumstances

John Foster

The quarterly meetings of the Irish Regional Committee through the 1970s and 80s frequently began with the chair reading the names of those members killed over previous weeks. The minutes for July 1975 record: 'Brother Duffy shot while coming from work (branch 11/60); Brother Convey died from gunshot wounds (branch 11/63); Brother McErlane assassinated (11/63 branch).' Six months later, the regional secretary opened the meeting by registering the Committee's outrage at 'the tragic events over the previous two nights and, in particular, the brutal murder of eight members of our union'.

The 'Troubles' dominated the lives of all in the North throughout these years. Amalgamated Transport and General Workers' Union (ATGWU) members were responsible for maintaining transport, the production and supply of food and for many public services, and they were drawn more or less equally from the two religious/cultural communities. Of the 3,000 killed, significant numbers came from the union.

The role of the ATGWU was not, however, a passive one. At the same time as defending the livelihoods of its members, the union also undertook a wider and more fundamental task: to defend the principles of labour and working-class unity. It did so in the most difficult of circumstances. Politically, it faced a wider institutional discrimination that sought to divide working people on access to employment, housing and education. Economically, through the 1960s, 70s and 80s, the North saw one of the biggest collapses in employment and industry anywhere in Europe.

The Radical Tradition of the ATGWU

The previous volume of this history has documented the role played by the union through the 1960s and early 70s and the traditions that it drew upon to do so. As a union originally based in the docks, in haulage, urban trades and general labouring, its members carried forward from the 1900s the radical commitments of the founding organisations of the Irish trade union movement.

The father of Joe Cooper, ATGWU commercial transport organiser through the 1970s and 80s and chair of Belfast Trades Council, had worked with both Larkin and Connolly in Belfast docks.[1] The pre-1949 regional secretary of the ATGWU (and previous leader of the Workers Union in Ireland), Sam Kyle, had worked with that union's founder, Tom Mann, and helped lead the 1919 Belfast general strike. He was still attending ATGWU functions in the North in the 1960s.[2] ATGWU member Betty Sinclair, Secretary of Belfast Trades Council in the mid-1970s and from a Protestant background, was originally a union activist among flax workers. She had been a Communist organiser and educator since the 1930s and tutored a new generation of activists in the 1940s, including Andy Holmes, who was chair of ATGWU through most of the 1970s. Others, like the previous ATGWU regional secretary Norman Kennedy, who retired in 1974, represented the traditions of the Northern Ireland Labour Party (NILP). This party was based among the Protestant working class, mainly in the industrial heartlands of Belfast, but represented its interests against the landlords and industrialists who dominated the Stormont parliament and ran the Ulster Unionist Party. In the early 1960s, NILP members had joined with others to support the demand for equal civil rights across both communities, and Kennedy himself had been a leading campaigner for the unity of the Irish unions within the Irish Congress of Trade Unions (ICTU). After securing this unity in 1959–1960, he denounced the Ulster Unionist Prime Minister Lord Brookeborough for refusing to recognise its Northern Ireland Committee (on the grounds that the ICTU was a 'foreign body'). Other ATGWU members came from the labour tradition within the republican community, as represented by Gerry Fitt and Paddy Devlin, or the left-wing republican clubs.

All these wider political traditions were present within the ATGWU. At the same time, the union's immediate task was to represent its tens of thousands of members who were first and foremost concerned with supporting themselves and their families through one of the most difficult and daunting periods of deindustrialisation anywhere in post-war Europe. Through the 1950s and 60s, unemployment had been around 7 per cent, three times the average in Britain. At its peak in 1981 it

---

1   Interviews with Kevin Cooper, 25 September 2020, and Frank Cooper, 9 February 2021, Unite archive, Holborn.

2   A newspaper cutting featuring a TGWU celebratory dinner with Frank Cousins in Lurgan Textile Hall in January 1960 records Sam Kyle, former regional secretary, as among those attending. Souvenir publication for the 34th Irish biennial conference, 18 June 1998, Craigavon District Office. I am indebted to Benny Lavery, chair of the 11/22 Lurgan branch for a copy.

reached 20 per cent (and up to 50 per cent in West Belfast and parts of Derry). It still remained at 17.6 per cent in 1986. By then manufacturing employment, supplying 172,000 jobs in 1974, had contracted to 103,000, and many of the overseas firms, bringing in up to 25,000 jobs on the basis of government subsidies in the 1960s, had departed. The biggest single manufacturing complex, the government-owned shipbuilding and aircraft plants at Harland & Wolff and Shorts, developed for armaments' production during the Second World War, had contracted from 50,000 jobs in the 1940s to fewer than 8,000 when finally privatised in 1989.[3] As manufacturing declined, public sector employment became more important – supplying up to 43 per cent of all jobs by 1986. Partly in consequence, the proportion of women workers increased from 42 per cent to 47 per cent.

Traditionally, the North had a higher level of unionisation than Britain or the Republic. In 1970, the levels were 54 per cent in the North, 52 per cent in the Republic and 49 per cent in Britain. There was also, traditionally, a higher level of industrial action. Still in the late 1970s the number of days lost per 100,000 was 664 as against 587 in Britain. But by 1987–1990 these positions had been reversed: 111 per 100,000 in the North against 149 in Britain – within a massive overall decline everywhere. And it was the ATGWU, as by far the biggest union in the North, that had the major responsibility for defending both the general interests of working people and, in the circumstances of the 1970s and 80s, seeking to sustain some measure of working-class unity.

The Battle to Maintain Workplace Unity

Unite History, volume 4 detailed the role of ATGWU members in defending the interests of working people. They did so both as shop stewards within workplaces and, more strategically, as officers of the union and of the Belfast Trades Council, which acted as a proxy for the Northern Ireland ICTU committee during its period of 'non-recognition' by Stormont. From the mid-1960s, ATGWU members played a leading role in developing the civil rights movement and in 1969–1970 in preventing sectarian conflict manifesting itself within workplaces – including some workplaces, such as Harland & Wolff, where there was a significant concentration of workers from the sectarian heartland of East Belfast. By and large, workplace unity was maintained through the years of escalating violence that followed

3 Mike Morrisey and Sean Morrisey, 'Northern Ireland: Why the Trade Unions Are Central', *Marxism Today*, November 1979; Henry Paterson, 'Northern Ireland Economy', in Arthur Augher and Duncan Morrow (eds), *Northern Ireland Politics* (Routledge, 2014); Emmet O'Connor, *A Labour History of Ireland 1824–2000* (UCD Press, 2011), pp.275–276.

– although not without targeted retaliation against those who rallied
support against sectarian initiatives.[4]

The biggest test came in May 1974 when hard-line elements in the
Ulster Unionist Party, allied with Ian Paisley, called a 'strike' to bring
down the power-sharing executive established in 1973. In reality this was
a lockout enforced by armed paramilitaries using hundreds of barricades to
block all access points across the province – with the British army, 50,000
strong, doing nothing to remove them. ATGWU members were among
those who attempted to break through the blockade with a march back
to work in the third week. Led by Andy Holmes, convener at Harland &
Wolff, and Norman Kennedy, regional secretary, two hundred marched
– with minimal military protection – through a hail of missiles. They
reached Harland & Wolff. A smaller march, led by ATGWU convener
Ernie McBride, reached Electronic Tabulators in unionist Cregagh. But
across the province the armed barricades remained. The power-sharing
executive fell a few days later.

The organisers of the lockout, operating under the title of the Ulster
Workers Council, declared victory. Over the following two months they
made a determined attempt to intervene in the trade union movement
itself. Under the name the Ulster Workers Association, they advanced a
manifesto calling for an annual conference of Northern Ireland trade unions
that would constitute an 'independent' Congress, demanded that all those
standing for election should declare their political positions, that officials
taking a nationalist position should be ousted and that Belfast Trades
Council should be 'reorganised'.[5] In Belfast's biggest industrial employer,
Harland & Wolff, a Workers Committee was established to campaign for
these demands.[6] But, with intimidation and an increased level of targeted
violence, these initiatives failed. Nowhere were existing shop stewards
replaced. Workers remained loyal to those who had previously represented
them. The 1974 Annual Report for Belfast Trades Council, signed by Joe
Cooper and Betty Sinclair, noted that 'the attempts to set up so-called
workers organisations to usurp the place and function of the official trade
union movement was not done just on the grounds of sectarianism. It is
the policy of the bosses and the upper class.' The report also noted the
personal cost. Although in the immediate aftermath of lockout the number
of delegates attending Trades Council meetings increased, 'violence, not
least the sectarian assassinations, drove it down again'.[7]

4 Interview with Eugene McGlone, 30 September 2020, Unite archive, Holborn.

5 *News Letter*, 12 August 1974, cutting in Trade Union Box 2, Belfast Linenhall
Library Political Collection.

6 Leaflet under the name of 'J. Best', Trade Union Box 1, Belfast Linenhall Library
Political Collection.

7 Belfast Trades Council, Annual Report 1974, Linenhall Library Political
Collection.

At the January 1975 meeting of the ATGWU, John Freeman, now the regional secretary, submitted a communication from Joe Cooper on behalf of the 11/52 and 11/65 branches, 'regarding the role of the trade union movement in the campaign for peace and the necessity for the unions to participate in such a campaign and that the Northern Ireland Committee of the Irish Congress of Trade Unions (NIC ICTU) be requested to convene a meeting of all shop stewards to initiate a campaign as outlined'.[8] At the April meeting, this was followed by a parallel resolution to the ICTU conference.

The October 1975 meeting considered a resolution received from the 11/50 Dungannon branch calling for the union to convene a meeting for all groups 'interested in ending sectarianism'. John Freeman responded that the necessary steps had already been taken. In response to ATGWU resolutions to NIC ICTU, the broad principles were being considered for a campaign by the trade union movement in Northern Ireland, which included a campaign directed against unemployment and sectarianism with the slogan 'Northern Irish trade unionists demand the right to live and work in peace.' The campaign would be launched by 'a large-scale rally'.

This initiative became the 'Better Life for All' campaign. It was launched in autumn 1975 and advanced six demands. These included the right to live free from violence and sectarian discrimination, the right to security of employment, the right to associate freely, the right to good housing and equality of educational opportunity and the right to adequate social services. Over the following months, this declaration was signed by 200,000 people across the North.[9]

Eighteen months later, in May 1977, Ian Paisley, jointly with Protestant paramilitaries and the right wing of the Ulster Unionist Party, launched another lockout. This was to compel the British government to restore the Stormont parliament – a parliament in which supporters of the Protestant ascendancy would be able to exercise absolute power. The NIC ICTU put out a statement calling for defiance, ending:

Let no one be under any doubt that there are enough guns and extremists in our midst to telescope into one week the 1,700 deaths and all the other evils of the last few years:
    Who would then be the victors?
    Who would claim the victory?
    For whom then would the bell toll?

8 ATGWU Regional Committee minutes, 5–6 January 1975, Unite Office, Antrim Road.
9 Ben D. Segal, 'Irish Trade Unions: Working for Peace in Northern Ireland', *Labour Studies Journal*, 1978, vol.2, no.3, pp.231–234.

After two weeks of attempted blockades, the armed lockout was abandoned. Key services, such as bus transport, were maintained – with ATGWU members, both Protestant and Catholic, in the front line. Among those killed was ATGWU bus driver Harry Bradshaw, listed in the June ATGWU minutes as 'shot in course of his employment'.[10] A commentary by a US labour correspondent stated: 'the courage of the [ICTU] committee was matched by the workers themselves who stayed at their workplaces despite the murder of several workers'.[11] The Annual Report of Belfast Trades Council paid tribute. It was

> to the credit of bus drivers that workers had public transport to get to work and indeed their heroism when they continued after one of their colleagues [...] was assassinated. [...] shop stewards in many areas braved the threats of intimidators [...] many were Trades Council delegates.[12]

Solidarity and the Politics of Class Unity

This reversal of what had happened in 1974 was not accidental. To a significant degree it stemmed from detailed organisational and political work undertaken by members of the ATGWU and allied unions in the Northern Ireland Committee of ICTU between 1974 and 1977. It had two components. One was the redevelopment of *community-based* trade union organisation across the province through the revival of Trades Councils. The other was to do so *politically*. The appeals for working-class unity were not made as pious calls for an end to religious divisions (and if they had been they would have had little effect). They were calls for class unity to halt the destruction of jobs, livelihoods and services on which local communities depended. And it was the ATGWU, as the North's biggest union, that was in the forefront of these actions – both supplying the financial and human resources for the redevelopment of a province-wide network of Trades Councils and the political direction needed to defend the economic and social interests of members – if necessary, as indeed it was, against the policies of the Labour administration in Westminster.

The first task of the ATGWU, after the defeat of the Conservative government in 1974, was to reverse the attacks on the North's large public sector and to demand the transfer to Northern Ireland of the new Labour legislation re-establishing trade union rights and providing workers with

---

10 ATGWU Quarterly Meeting minute, June 1977, Unite Office, Antrim Road.
11 Segal, 'Irish Trade Unions'.
12 Belfast Trades Council, Annual Report 1977, Linenhall Library Political Collection.

new statutory powers over health and safety. This, jointly with the NIC ICTU, was largely, although not entirely, achieved. In 1974–1975, in common with the TGWU at British level, the Regional Committee also voted to campaign against membership of the Common Market – noting in particular its potential impact on employment in the North's large agricultural sector. In July 1976, it went further in defending class interests and defied Jack Jones and the NEC to do so. It voted to condemn national union policy of support for the Labour government's Social Contract. In response to a motion from Belfast's biggest branch, 11/30, it voted 'to deplore the action of the NEC for its support and endorsement of TUC's part in the Social Contract for 1976–77'.

At least part of the background to this was the particularly sharp impact on the North of the new monetarist policies introduced in early 1976 by Dennis Healey. In April 1976, the 11/30 branch had submitted a motion to the Irish Committee that it was 'horrified with the effect of government policy on employment in Northern Ireland. Recent decisions in relation to RAF Sydenham, RAF Aldergrove and REME Antrim linked with the closure of IEL, Heysham Ferry and Rolls Royce and the failure to include Harland & Wolff and the NI aerospace industry in the overall strategy for these industries demonstrate a failure to appreciate the grave situation' in the North. Another Belfast branch, 11/38, expressed 'deep concern' at a further deterioration in unemployment. 'The latest measures by Dennis Healey are designed to increase unemployment rather than reduce it in Northern Ireland.' A further motion from 11/38 condemned the cuts in public spending, in education and in transport, and noted that while these services were being cut there was no restriction on the profits of major companies such as the General Electric Company.

All these motions were passed without opposition. As well as matching the grim economic realities of 1975–1976, they also reflected the higher levels of both unionisation and industrial action in the North. Despite the growing scale of sectarian polarisation during what were very difficult years, collective union actions, on jobs, conditions and pay, still exceeded that across the water in Britain. The politics of class unity which this militancy expressed provided an essential unifying focus across the union's membership. Without it, and the accompanying policies, the cross-sectarian Better Life for All campaign, as launched in autumn 1975, would have had little effect.

At the same time, there was also, as has been noted, another key component. This was organisational – and human. It was also one in which the ATGWU had a particularly important role. It was the re-establishment and strengthening of the North's Trades Councils.

Apart from Belfast, and even this was under pressure in the mid-1970s, most of the North's traditionally strong array of Trades Councils had either ceased to function by the mid-1970s or survived only as result of the determination of a handful of individuals. Yet Trades Councils possessed a potential for local community mobilisation not available even to the biggest unions. Trades Councils brought together a range of unions – often of varying social and religious backgrounds – with a responsibility for developing, and campaigning for, policies that represented working people collectively as a class in the locality. They embodied solidarity between unions as well as with the many working people then out of employment and the wider class interests of the local community as a whole.

The April 1975 meeting of the Regional Committee backed a motion from the 11/50 Dungannon branch calling for a meeting of other local branches to 'discuss the various social and economic problems which are facing the people of this area'. A year later, the April 1976 Regional Committee, in response to motions from branches in the Portadown, Lurgan and Craigavon areas calling for affiliation to the new Craigavon Trades Council, 'noted with pleasure the establishment of Trades Councils throughout Northern Ireland arising from the Better Life for All campaign' and authorised the regional secretary 'to affiliate the Union to Trades Councils as they are progressively established arising from the Better Life for All campaign'.

Under the circumstances of the time, these initiatives depended on strong individuals able to provide the local leadership needed to bridge the two religious communities – and do so against targeted personal violence.

Building Class Unity Locally

In Portadown, Lurgan and Craigavon, a key figure was Dessie Henderson.[13] These three towns were strung along an eight-mile stretch of road nicknamed 'the mid-Ulster murder triangle'. Portadown was 90 per cent Protestant, Lurgan 90 per cent Catholic and Craigavon, a largely abortive 'new town', midway between them. Dessie was born in Portadown in 1956. As a Catholic in a Protestant town, he experienced institutional discrimination at first hand. His street was 'Catholic', next to the railway. It had minimal amenities and the house was regularly visited by the Royal Ulster Constabulary to check on his father, the leader of a Hibernian band. His schooling did not extend beyond O levels as there was no Catholic secondary school in Portadown. He started work as a labourer – but received lower wages than similar Protestant school leavers. He left in protest. He had, with his father, taken part in civil rights marches and as a teenager had, like many others, spent time in Crumlin Road prison. He could at that stage have been consumed by the sectarian conflict but he got taken on as labourer at the Metal Box factory, one of the incoming multinationals and 100 per cent trade union.

---

13 Interview with Dessie Henderson, 22 July 2021, Unite archive, Holborn.

It was there he became involved with the ATGWU – remembering, particularly, the ATGWU organiser Sam Best, from a Protestant background but committed to trade union values and as a result under attack by paramilitaries.[14] He also remembers the very strong separation of the mental worlds of the workplace, 'where there was some feeling of common interest and sticking together', and outside, where religious allegiance took over. Despite his youth, he quickly became a shop steward – learning the need to be seen to be equally protecting all workers and, no less important, that it was the active struggle against injustice that united workers, building an understanding of common interest and of the solidarity needed to secure it. Words themselves meant very little. During the 1977 paramilitary lockout, he managed, even in Protestant Portadown, to evade road blocks and, as with some others, get into work.

It was in these circumstances that the new Craigavon Trades Council had come into being in 1976, bringing together trade unionists from the three towns, and from the mid-1970s involved in an intensifying struggle against industrial closures and unemployment. By 1980, Dessie Henderson remembers addressing a rally of many thousands in Craigavon against plant closures and unemployment.

Newry was 20 miles to the south-east, on the coast. The town originally developed around the docks at the end of the River Bann canal. Once a centre of the flax industry, the old factories had been partially replaced in the 1960s by incoming multinational plants. But the town still suffered very high levels of unemployment. It was largely Catholic in a border area with a patchwork of Catholic and Protestant communities. It was here, in January 1976, that over two successive days, eight members of the union were killed, in the first case Catholics and the second Protestants.

Tom Moore was then chair of Newry Trades Council and somewhat older than Dessie Henderson.[15] Born in 1945, he originally trained as a missionary but then joined the civil rights movement and was interned through the early 1970s. He eventually got employment in a meat factory, FMC, joined the ATGWU, became a shop steward and then an organiser. As chair of Newry Trades Council at the time of the 1976 killings, he helped organise a mass cross-sectarian rally, involving union and civic leaders as well as local clergy, under the banner of NIC ICTU and the Better Life for All campaign. It was the scale and effectiveness of this cross-community initiative which was one reason why Paisley's attempted lockout 15 months later received almost no support in Newry.

14 Sam Best's life is recorded, along with other ATGWU members from the Lurgan area, in the souvenir publication produced for the 34th Irish biennial conference, 18 June 1998.
15 Interview with Tom Moore, 20 July 2021, Unite archive, Holborn.

Sectarian tensions remained.[16] But a measure of cross-community class unity was sustained. The Trades Council had led a series of struggles which united local trade unionists – in defence of health services, against industrial closures or against local anti-union employers, as at Edward Haughey's Norbrook Laboratories. Also important was the development of links with other neighbouring Trades Councils in communities of differing religious composition, such as Craigavon and Armagh, and the practice of holding joint May Day demonstrations.

Far to the west, in Enniskillen, there was a similar story. There an operating Trades Council had survived – but it was largely through the efforts of one individual, the local ATGWU organiser, Jimmy Brown, another pupil of Betty Sinclair. However, the mid-1970s saw a change. A trio of new activists was recruited: Jim Quinn, Tommy Campbell and Davie Kettlys, all tutored by Jimmy Brown, and, between them, carried forward a strengthened Trades Council into the next century.

Enniskillen Trades Council had been formed in 1919, a period of trade union growth and mobilisation across Ireland and with the lead taken by the National Amalgamated Union of Labour, a precursor of the TGWU, organising building labourers, agricultural workers and general workers in a period of temporary full employment.[17] The new Trades Council recruits in the 1970s, all ATGWU members, also came in a period of expansion for the ATGWU locally – with the Regional Committee agreeing in April 1977 to the appointment of an additional local officer to service the new members. Their involvement in the Trades Council stemmed from spontaneous reactions against the manifest injustices experienced locally – political and occupational. But it would not have crystalised into effective leadership without repeated political discussion led by Jimmy Brown putting an alternative class perspective, an understanding of the need for non-sectarian unity to secure basic social change.

By the later 1970s, with Tommy Campbell as Trades Council secretary, the new recruits were producing a monthly local paper, challenging unfair employment practices, recruiting more young people, expounding the need for united working-class action, and as a result being seen to provide a significant local alternative to sectarian politics. Always, however, this was based in practical campaigning – on unemployment, benefits, housing – against the increasing tide of workplace closures and, more widely, against Conservative government policy. It also provided the base for wider links with other Trades Councils in Tyrone and Derry focusing on the class issues as posed by the Better Life for All campaign.

16 Interviews with Tommy Campbell, 8 July 2021, and Jim Quinn, 9 July 2021, Unite archive, Holborn.

17 Jim Quinn, *Labouring Beside Loch Erne: A Study of the Fermanagh Labour Movement 1826–1932* (Umiskin Press, 2019).

TGWU Debates British Government Policy on Ireland

This complex work of sustaining class unity in the most difficult of circumstances was the background to the political debates on the TGWU policies on Ireland that took place at biennial conferences in 1977, 1979 and 1981.

At each conference, motions came forward, usually from branches in Region 1 (London and SE), calling on the union to demand the withdrawal of British troops and a declaration of intent by Britain to end its occupation of the North. At each, representatives of the ATGWU, led by John Freeman, opposed. They advanced instead the programme of the Better Life for All campaign and its successor, as adopted in 1980.

The 1979 biennial conference saw John Freeman and others from Ireland arguing against a series of speakers from Regions 1, 4 (Wales) and 6 (North West and Merseyside).[18] Freeman made clear the union's support for the right to self-determination and opposition to the use of torture and intimidation by any state. But he then warned against motions mandating the union to support policies that would align it to just one section, and a minority one, of the population in the North. 'The evil of divisions amongst the working people of Northern Ireland will find cure and correction in the pursuit of working class objectives as defined in the six points of the Better Life for All campaign.' He then went on to quote James Connolly that the immediate and long-term solution to Northern Ireland's problems lies 'with the interests of the working class'.

> The working class in Ireland through the Trade Union Movement continue the struggle against calculated sectarian violence and para-military gangs who seek to create inter-community tension and polarisation in order to attain domination over their respective communities. [...] Faced with enormous difficulties, the Transport and General Workers Union in Northern Ireland has given and will continue to give leadership and will continue to instil political courage into a confused but far from demoralised working class who have been manipulated in the past by politicians for unscrupulous non-working class objectives.

He was followed by Andy Holmes from Harland & Wolff:

> [E]motive statements are filling our grave yards in Belfast. [...] our job is to weld the working class of Northern Ireland together and when we are welding them we will have to weld Orangemen

---

18 Transcript of speeches at 1979 biennial conference, February 1980, National Library of Scotland, Campaign for Democratic Rights in Northern Ireland (CDRNI) papers, Gallacher Collection.

and Nationalists. [...] An attempted coup was made in 1977 but because of the hard work that our own union in particular have done [...] we defeated the coup. We did not defeat it without losses.

Eugene McGlone then appealed to conference: 'we go back to Ireland on Monday, not you, so you allow us to decide on which way we run our affairs; but you support us and support us strongly [...] by giving Northern Ireland a better life for all'.

The executive composite, eventually passed unanimously, called for support for the Better Life campaign, demanded a Bill of Rights protecting civil liberties, endorsed the Quigley Report on the economy of the North – which called for government investment in the North supported by strengthened economic links with both the Republic and with Britain – and further demanded 'direct state investment in the manufacturing sector' and the development of a 'Nationalised sector'.

In summer 1979, delegates returning to the North were faced with a new Conservative government in Westminster with an explicitly anti-working-class agenda: enforcing absolute cuts in public expenditure, up to 3 per cent, at a time when inflation was already running at over 8 per cent. For a period, direct class mobilisation in Northern Ireland did increase. On 2 April 1980, a half-day general strike took place across the North – with the Northern Ireland CBI reporting a range of major firms being closed down for a full day. Some ten thousand workers massed in front of Belfast's City Hall – with trade unionists marching into the centre in symbolic unity from respectively Protestant and Catholic neighbourhoods. Four weeks later, the Belfast May Day was one of the biggest for some years.[19]

But this revived unity against an anti-working-class Conservative government depended on a delicate balance between levels of employment, unionisation and class mobilisation. While unemployment did increase in the late 1970s, so had union membership and trade union activity, as well as class-oriented community mobilisation. Closures and cuts were resisted. Catholics and Protestants resisted in tandem – and the arrival of a Tory government in Westminster temporarily strengthened an explicitly class agenda. This mobilisation did not necessarily reverse the momentum of sectarian division. But it did limit it. Soon, however, the process reversed itself. The scale of unemployment, up to 20 per cent in 1981, the loss of union membership, and particularly the closure of plants in some of the best unionised sectors (such as synthetic fibres and engineering) seriously sapped the ability of the trade union movement to mobilise and develop wider solidarity.

---

19 ICTU flyer for 2 April 1980, Trade Union Box 1 and Belfast Trades Council, Annual Report 1980, Belfast Linenhall Library Political Collection; CDRNI, Bulletin 1, May 1980, National Library of Scotland, Gallacher Collection.

A Delicate Balance: Employment, Unionisation and
Class Mobilisation

The January 1981 quarterly committee's main agenda item under the regional secretary's report was 'loss of membership'. 'Many members spoke at large on the very serious situation and the need for all trade unionists to involve themselves in the fight against the present government's policies.' The loss of membership also required agreement on the need 'to reduce expenditure'. Six months later, in July 1981, the committee noted unemployment 'growing by the day'. By April 1982, Harland & Wolff itself was under threat and John Freeman described the situation as 'very bleak'.[20]

These same years, 1981–1983, also saw Ian Paisley seeking to consolidate his grip over Protestant communities ahead of new elections. While the Provisional IRA worked towards a new electoral front, successive hunger strikes by Provisional IRA prisoners provided a new focus for community mobilisation on behalf of Sinn Fein.

In response, the April 1981 meeting of the Regional Committee agreed that the region's Education and Research officer, Sean Morrissey, should take responsibility for launching a professionally produced regional journal for the wider dissemination of ATGWU perspectives – provided branches were able to guarantee sales and financial support. However, the October 1981 meeting heard a report that branches did not see themselves able to guarantee the necessary sales. The proposal was abandoned. It is also clear that wider community initiatives through Trades Council activity were also facing increasing difficulties. The January 1982 meeting of the Regional Committee agreed a motion from the 11/98 branch in Belfast, largely public sector workers, for a meeting of all Trades Council delegates from across the North to assess the problems. Arising from this meeting and its bleak assessment, the April 1982 meeting agreed to organise a school for Trades Council delegates. By the autumn of 1982, John Freeman was again reporting 'very serious problems confronting the union' in terms of the loss of members and funds. January 1983 saw the Regional Committee calling off plans for a People's March for Jobs as 'impracticable in view of the poor response throughout Northern Ireland regarding unemployment demonstrations'. October 1983 saw the regional secretary again calling for a recruitment campaign and 'rebuilding the trade union movement'.[21]

Locally, the Trades Councils were struggling. Ballymena, for instance, refounded in 1980 as result of intervention by the NIC of the ICTU, secured

---

20 ATGWU Regional Committee minutes, January 1981, July 1981 and April 1982, Unite Office, Antrim Road.

21 ATGWU Regional Committee minutes, April 1981, October 1981, January, April, October 1982 and October 1983, Unite Office, Antrim Road.

initial affiliations by seven unions and nine branches. Initial attendances secured up to 20 delegates (three from the ATGWU) – despite 'people frightened to go out'. But the Council's last AGM was 1983. The meeting in 1984 failed to secure a forum.[22] Even the relatively strong Councils in Enniskillen/Fermanagh were finding things difficult. The AGM for 1982 reported that 'over the past year we again faced a political stalemate within Northern Ireland and a backward retreat to sectarian politics and an outburst of the most barbaric violence'.[23] Enniskillen's 'week of action' on unemployment in April 1981 had secured only a 'very poor turnout'. Belfast Trades Council, along with NIC ICTU and affiliated unions, managed to secure reasonable attendance for the April 1981 week of action jointly with Trades Councils from North Down, Lisburn and Newtownabbey, and a good May Day to mark its centenary. Its overall assessment, however, was that the 'hunger strikes […] polarised still further the community and sharpened sectarian divisions […] a hardening of attitudes with little common ground'. The Trades Council itself was still able to maintain a relatively strong attendance, of between 50 and 60 delegates in the first half of the 1980s, but increasingly these delegates were drawn from the public sector. In 1983, two younger ATGWU members, Brian Campfield and Liam McBrinn, took over as, respectively, secretary and president. Their report for that year noted 'the working class remains seriously divided' amid a 'horrifying growth in sectarian violence'. By the later 1980s, Belfast Trades Council was itself reporting a decline in attendance by delegates.[24]

Yet the work of core trade union activists in the ATGWU continued. The ATGWU, along with the NIC ICTU, was instrumental in the establishment of the People's College in 1983 to promote cross-community trade union education, and Tommy Campbell from Enniskillen became its first development officer.[25] In 1985, the ATGWU, along with Belfast Trades Council and the NIC ICTU, helped establish and fund the Belfast Unemployed Workers' Centre – based in central Belfast, with equal access from Protestant and Catholic areas, and becoming a centre for cross-community campaigning and discussion.[26] In workplaces, ATGWU

---

22 *Ballymena Observer*, 27 November 1980 and papers of Ballymena Trades Council for 2 December 1980, 16 December 1980 and notes of successive meetings, Trade Union Box 2, Belfast Linenhall Library Political Collection.

23 Enniskillen Trades Council, Annual Report, March 1982, Trade Union Box 1, Belfast Linenhall Library Political Collection.

24 Belfast Trades Council, Annual Reports 1981, 1983, 1987 and 1988 for decreased attendance, Linen Hall Library Political Collection.

25 Interview with Tommy Campbell, 8 July 2021; ATGWU Regional minutes, October 1983; Belfast Trades Council, Annual Report 1985, Linen Hall Library Political Collection.

26 Belfast Trades Council, Annual Report 1985, Linen Hall Library Political Collection.

stewards were active in challenging assertions of sectarian control. In Harland & Wolff in 1987 it was the ATGWU shop steward Joe Law who led the successful, but initially very difficult, challenge to the display of loyalist regalia. Three years later it was Joe Law who became a key figure in the establishment of Northern Ireland's first explicitly anti-sectarian campaigning organisation, CounterAct.[27] The resulting working-class dialogues, focusing on the unity of working-class interests and direct and immediate needs, increasingly extended into the contested territories of working-class unionism and working-class republicanism. By the mid- to later 1980s, there were the beginnings of more active links and left-wing engagement between some elements of both Catholic and Protestant paramilitaries.[28] It was on the basis of these developments that the 1989 Annual Report of Belfast Trades Council reflected a 'new optimism': the redevelopment within the organised working class of a willingness to 'struggle, which has not been visible since the early days of the Thatcher reign [...] on NHS privatisation, the Poll Tax, erosion of civil liberties and policy on public sector pay' – and, possibly of particular significance, against the privatisation of the unionist bastions, Shorts and Harland & Wolff.[29]

In all this, the radical traditions of the ATGWU, mentioned at the beginning of the chapter, continued to play a vital role – an understanding that class politics, the need to challenge an exploitative system as argued by Connolly and Tom Mann, played an essential part in building the wider unity needed for effective trade union struggle.

27 Brian Campfield and Jimmy Kelly, *Essays in Honour of Joe Law* (Belfast Trades Council, 2019), p.3.
28 Mel Corry, 'Confronting the Legacy of the Past' and Sophie Long, 'Loyalism and Labour', in Campfield and Kelly, *Essays in Honour of Joe Law*.
29 Belfast Trades Council, Annual Report 1989, Linen Hall Library Political Collection.

9

Scotland: Where Solidarity Defeated Thatcherism

John Foster

By 1986, unemployment in Scotland had reached almost half a million – up by 350,000 since 1971. In manufacturing alone, 200,000 jobs had been lost and already by the early 1980s a fifth of all school leavers were on the dole and many others on short-term job-creation schemes. Coal mining, the mainstay of many of Scotland's rural communities, was virtually wiped out by the end of the decade. Many other jobs had gone in the newly privatised utilities: transport, gas, oil, chemicals, communications, airlines and shipbuilding, as well as in local government.[1]

Yet up to this point, Scotland's trade union membership had held up relatively well. It was still just above a million at the end of the 1980s – only 200,000 down from its peak in the early 1970s. And, more significant still, and strongly against the trend elsewhere, Scotland had moved politically to the left. Earlier in the century, Scotland's politics had generally been to the right – with the Conservatives usually dominant electorally up to 1959. But in 1979, when the Conservatives won across Britain by a landslide, Labour was 11 per cent ahead in Scotland. In 1982, Labour was 8 per cent ahead and in 1987, 12 per cent. The rise of the SNP had a role in this – probably taking somewhat more votes from the Tories than Labour at this stage. But not by much. In the 1997 election, the Conservatives were wiped out and left with no seats at all.

This chapter seeks to understand how this happened: why, in stark contrast to developments elsewhere, the values and politics of Scotland's trade union and labour movement became more, not less, dominant through the late 1970s and 80s. In this examination, the role of the TGWU quickly becomes apparent. It did not act alone. It worked in concert with other unions. But it played a key role on a number of fronts.

1 Stephen Boyle, *Scotland's Economy: Claiming the Future*, 2nd ed. (Verso, 1989), pp.5–7; Christopher Harvie, 'Scotland after 1978', in R.A. Houston and William Knox (eds), *New Penguin History of Scotland* (Penguin, 2002), pp.494–531.

It was the main union, along with the engineers, in mobilising resistance to industrial closures. It led the opposition to privatisation in the public sector – in transport, power and housing – and, as the dominant union in commercial road transport, its refusal to cross picket lines was also important for solidarity action in support of other unions – with the miners in 1984–1985 and print workers in 1986.

In addition, the TGWU was also to the fore in two other critical areas. One was the campaign for a Scottish parliament. The other was its understanding of the importance of what today would be described as 'community organising'. Politically, it was the TGWU that led the fight for the establishment of representative institutions in Scotland – specifically on terms that would ensure the defence of working-class interests. Over these years, the TGWU had two outstanding leaders. One was Alex Kitson, previously general secretary of the Scottish Commercial Motormen's Union. After the merger in 1971, Kitson served as executive secretary and then assistant general secretary of the TGWU at British level and remained throughout a leading figure in the Scottish Labour Party and on the General Council of the Scottish Trades Union Congress (STUC). The other figure was Hugh Wyper, previously secretary of Glasgow Trades Council, who served as TGWU Scottish regional secretary from 1978 to 1986. Both Kitson and Wyper were committed and outspoken supporters of a Scottish parliament – seeing it as an essential democratic platform for rallying forces for the defence of Scotland's economy and mobilising pressure at British level against the dominance of big business and finance. Their ability, in these years, to win first the STUC and then the Labour Party to champion this position was one key factor in the growing political dominance of Labour in Scottish politics.

The August 1974 issue of the Scottish Region's journal, *The Highway*, was devoted almost entirely to outlining the case for a legislative assembly for Scotland. The previous April issue had carried an article from Jim Sillars, then Labour MP for Ayr, condemning the Scottish Labour Party for failing to give full support to an elected Scottish Assembly. In the August issue, both Kitson and Ray MacDonald, Scottish regional secretary up to 1978, stressed the union's unqualified backing for an 'elected legislative assembly' – with its determination to campaign for it 'reaffirmed only a few weeks ago'. The centre-page feature continued:

We shall not build a socialist society simply by saying over and over that the purpose of the Labour Party is to bring about a fundamental and irreversible shift in the balance of power and wealth in favour of working people. That outcome can only be secured when we change the nature and form of society, extending the forms of government in a way that gives working people a fuller understanding of the true nature of power and a greater say in all affairs [...] to develop their strength and gain experience.

On the back page, Alex Kitson explained why a Scottish Assembly was needed immediately, to take 'vital decisions concerning the Scottish economy', and attacked current regional policy directed from London as 'incoherent and unplanned'.[2]

'Community organising' was particularly associated with Hugh Wyper. Between 1964 and 1978, as secretary of Glasgow Trades Council, Wyper had been instrumental in setting up trade union community centres and social clubs across the Glasgow area – in parallel to the 'miners' welfares' that had long provided the social and political focus for mining communities. In the late 1970s and 80s, trade union centres became bases for a wider network of unemployment centres, operating with support from the STUC, and often more directly, in terms of financial support from the TGWU and local Trades Councils. These centres, in turn, became the organising hubs for resistance to closures and for support for workers in dispute, most notably for the miners in 1984–1985.

While by no means unique to Scotland, they were also, and critically, able to draw upon considerable financial support from Scottish urban and regional authorities – in this period almost all under Labour control. These local authorities, particularly the new regional councils, still possessed considerable financial resources. They also exercised a significant level of political autonomy. And, unlike ministers in the Tory-controlled Scottish Office, they possessed a direct democratic mandate.

Together, these union–community alliances, underpinned by financial support from local government, posed a formidable organisational challenge to the Conservatives in Scotland – reinforced by the political demand for Scottish devolution. In turn, Conservative ministers in St Andrew's House sought to target both local authorities and community organisations. Sometimes these attacks, as in the privatisation of home ownership and other council services, although resisted, were successively forced through – with long-term detrimental effects. Other attacks turned out to be dangerously counter-productive. This was particularly so for the attempt to impose a poll tax in the period from 1987 to 1990. Designed to undermine Labour in local government, this resulted in levels of mass civil disobedience not seen since the 1920s. Equally, there was some success in the resistance to the privatisation of bus transport, notably in the Lothians, the country's second largest urban area. And, uniquely in Scotland, water privatisation had to be abandoned in face of popular resistance and a referendum held by Strathclyde Regional Council, representing well over a third of Scotland's total population.

This chapter will examine in turn the privatisations in housing and bus transport, the resistance to industrial closures and the union's wider commitment to community campaigning and industrial and political solidarity.

2 *The Highway*, April 1974 and August 1974.

Resistance to Privatisation

The Tories' first and probably most strategic attack was on council housing. Already in 1974 the Tory party had identified council housing as a major cause of their political and electoral defeat that year – particularly in Scotland. As a 1974 Conservative Party research publication put it: 'Simply by visiting Glasgow one can see life as it will be throughout the country if the trend to council housing continues. Housing in industrial Scotland has much in common with that in many Iron Curtain countries [...] housing has frozen class divisions.'[3]

While the attack on council housing had in fact begun before – with the 1973 Housing Finance Act – a new and much more determined assault began within months of the Tories' election victory. In the autumn of 1979, legislation was introduced enabling tenants to buy houses at highly discounted prices. By October 1980, the 'right to buy' was in place.

The initial take-up was slow. Buying a council house was widely viewed as anti-social behaviour in working-class communities. But by the mid- and later 1980s it was beginning to make inroads. Stevie Dillon, then a painter in Monklands' 'direct works' department, remembers significant numbers of houses starting to disappear from the painters' lists in streets with houses in the best conditions – resulting in consequent cuts in the workforce.[4] At this point, in the later 1980s, a further blow fell. Compulsory competitive tendering was imposed in the wake of the 1986 EU Single Market Act, itself largely drafted by Tory ministers. Big UK contractors moved in, displacing both 'direct works' staff and small local firms. In Paisley, Eric Blackburn, another painter, and at the time the union convener for 'direct works', remembers the united response from trade unions and the local left-wing Paisley District Council.[5] The council, with union support, organised large-scale factory-level production of key units such as roofing and windows and was able to win the contracts and expand the workforce. Later, this unity, involving local tenants' associations and Paisley and District Trades Council, of which Eric was then chair, enabled a narrow victory in the vote against the full privatisation of council housing. At roughly the same time, in North Lanarkshire, Stevie Dillon, then union convener for 'direct works', organised a successful resistance to its privatisation by the council – marching 1,000 workers in a surprise assault on the council headquarters, brushing aside the police and occupying the buildings. The Council leader resigned within the week and full privatisation was abandoned.

---

3 Bob Patten, *The Eclipse of the Private Landlord: A Study of the Consequences* (Conservative Political Centre for the Junior Carlton Club, 1974).

4 Interview with Stevie Dillon, 28 October 2021, Unite Oral History Archive.

5 Interview with Eric Blackburn, 21 November 2021, Unite Oral History Archive.

Bus privatisation was initiated by the Tories' 1985 Transport Act. This Act, coming into force in October 1986, enabled private companies to launch routes wherever they wanted as long as they notified the Traffic Commissioner. It also strictly limited the subsidies that local councils could provide for publicly provided services and split the existing public sector National Bus Company into 70 separate entities, that had to be self-financing.

The TGWU organised a strong and partly successful fightback. Lothian Buses remains today the only major bus company in Britain that is ultimately publicly owned and controlled. This outcome was the result of a determined and strategic campaign of resistance. The key factor was the unity between TGWU members across the Lothians, led by full-time officer Charlie Ripley, support from the Labour-controlled Lothian Regional Council and Alex Kitson's role on the board of Lothian Regional Transport, which he joined immediately he retired as TGWU deputy general secretary in 1986. Kitson ensured a united regional opposition from the Labour Party, not always the case elsewhere, and a concerted and legally effective campaign through the courts and in parliament. Repeated attempts by the big business-owned First Bus to grab routes and custom were boycotted by the public – eventually resulting in the closure of their Dalkeith headquarters. Today, the publicly controlled Lothian Buses continues to provide lower fares, better buses, better services and better terms and conditions of employment than any of the private monopolists – and still returns large dividends to the local councils.[6]

In the west, Strathclyde Regional Transport was broken into three groups. The biggest, initially renamed Clydeside 2000, temporarily became an employee-led buy-out. Headed by a former Glasgow bus garage TGWU convener, Eddie Cassidy, this successfully provided services for the bulk of Clydeside for the two years from 1987. However, in order to buy the company, the workers had both to raise funds from themselves and then, to meet the full valuation, to take on a substantial loan from a major Scottish bank. Suddenly, after two years of viable and effective operation, and without warning or good reason, the bank demanded the money back. Clydeside 2000 had then to sell its assets. The big private companies took over its routes and the employees were transferred.[7] It is very clear, looking at directorships of the private companies promoted in this process, that Edinburgh-based joint stock banks and merchant banks had close political involvement from the very beginning.

6 Interview with Irene Kitson, board member of Lothian Buses, January 2022, Unite Oral History Archive.

7 Interview with Eddie Cassidy, who led the employee buy-out, December 2021, Unite Oral History Archive.

In Fife, Archie Low, convener of the Cowdenbeath and then Lochgelly garages, also a member of the TGWU Scottish and British Passenger Group executive, formed alliances with Fife Council and local MPs Gordon Brown and Harry McLeish, and kept Fife Regional Buses public until 1990 – with some of the best terms and conditions (and fares and services) in Britain. Then the Scottish Office intervened. It demanded that the company was put up for public auction, with Stagecoach as the preferred bidder. Parliamentary interventions and legal action by the TGWU stayed any handover until a High Court appeal. But again the award went to Stagecoach. After the takeover, the union successfully maintained the struggle for existing conditions and fully defended the final salary pension. But public control was lost.[8]

Closures

In parallel with this tide of privatisation, which also included key industrial assets such as BP's oil refining complex at Grangemouth in 1987, the 1980s saw a tidal wave of plant closures on a scale well beyond what had been experienced in the 1970s.

Within weeks of the Tory election victory, closures were announced at three major US-owned plants: the Singer Sewing Machine factory in Clydebank, Massey Ferguson in Kilmarnock and Goodyear Tyres in Drumchapel, Glasgow. This timing was at least in part a result of the removal of Bruce Millan and other Labour Party ministers from the Scottish Office – ending the danger of political intervention exposing the closures as a consequence of global corporate restructuring and not, as they were posed, as the result of local production problems. Each closure had devastating effects on local communities. Massey Ferguson, the only producer of combine harvesters in Britain, robbed the Ayrshire economy of 2,000 jobs, Singer stripped away even more – over 4,000 from Clydebank – and, just across the Glasgow boundary, Goodyear took another 800.[9]

In each case, campaigns were mounted, with local community support. At Massey Ferguson and Singer, the dominant union was the AEUW. In Goodyear, it was the TGWU, and here negotiations were led by Ray MacDonald and Hugh Wyper. As with Singer, the Goodyear management demanded changes in working conditions that they knew would be unacceptable and then used the lure of redundancy payments to split the workforce and enforce closure. The following year it was the turn of the

---

8 Interview with Archie Low, December 2021, Unite Oral History Archive.

9 Michael McDermot, 'Foreign Disinvestment and Employee Disclosure and Consultation in the UK 1978–1985', PhD thesis, Glasgow University, 1986; Simon Henderson, 'Multinational Closure and the Case of Massey Ferguson, Kilmarnock', *Industrial Relations Journal*, 1984, vol.15, no.4, pp.17–27.

Paisley area. The giant Peugeot car plant at Linwood, previously Rootes and then Chrysler, had 7,500 employees in 1979 – although already reduced to 5,000 by 1981. Most were TGWU members. Here, the initial response was to resist. Again, however, the offer of redundancy payments split the workforce, and closure was agreed against the advice of the union and the shop stewards' Action Committee.[10]

It was later in 1981, as unemployment increased to levels not seen since the 1930s, that resistance began to stiffen. In Greenock, another US multinational, Lee Jeans, looked for closure. The mainly female workforce decided to resist and occupied – although with limited support from their union, the Tailors and Garment Workers, which seems to have been concerned about the new Tory penalties for 'illegal' action. The workers continued their occupation for seven months, holding ransom stocks of materials worth millions, and sustained by support from other workplaces, the community, the STUC and unions including the TGWU. Ultimately, Lee Jeans agreed a management buy-out that saved over 80 of the jobs – with the workers switching their union memberships to the TGWU in light of its consistent support throughout.[11] This success, although limited, probably had a significant impact on the decision of women workers at Lovable Brassiere in Cumbernauld to mount a similar resistance later the same year. Then, in early 1982, at Plessey Capacitators in Bathgate, another mainly female workforce also occupied when Plessey sought to close the plant. In this case, the occupiers won an important legal judgment exploiting the differences between the English and Scots laws of trespass. This prevented eviction and effectively forced Plessey to sell the occupied factory to another firm, preserving some of the jobs and setting important legal precedents for subsequent occupations.[12] This was certainly the case in April 1983 for the mainly male engineering workers at Timex's Milton of Craigie plant in Dundee. They occupied to halt closure by the US owners and won qualified victory with a transfer to the firm's local Camperdown plant.[13]

10 Alison Gilmore, 'Examining the "Hard Boiled Bunch": Work Culture and Industrial Relations at Linwood Car Plant, 1963–1981', PhD thesis, Glasgow University, 2009.

11 Margaret Robertson and A. Clark, '"We Were the Ones Really Doing Something about It": Gender and Mobilisation against Factory Closure', *Work, Employment and Society*, 2018, vol.32, no.2, pp.336–344.

12 Patricia Findlay, 'Resistance, Restructuring and Gender: The Plessey Occupation', in A. Dickson and D. Judge, *The Politics of Industrial Closure* (Macmillan, 1987); Kenneth Miller, '*Plessey Co. Ltd.* v. *Wilson*', *Industrial Law Journal*, 1982, vol.11, no.1, pp.115–117.

13 J. Phillips, J. Tomlinson and V. Wright, 'Defending the Right to Work: The 1983 Timex Workers' Occupation in Dundee', *Labour History Review*, 2021, vol.86, no.1, pp.63–90.

The most celebrated occupation was that by the workers at the giant Caterpillar plant in 1986–1987 – in an ex-mining area of Lanarkshire. It was also the most overtly political. Caterpillar had secured major government grants earlier in 1986 to redevelop the factory, the biggest complex in Europe in terms of floor space. The formal launch was attended by the Scottish Secretary of State, Malcolm Rifkind, keen to assert his administration's commitment to Scottish industry. Then three months later, the firm announced closure – just five months ahead of a general election. The workforce occupied, capturing the state-of-the art capital equipment which the company urgently wanted to transfer to plants elsewhere. The occupation galvanised the wider trade union movement and local communities – still angry at the virtual martial law imposed during the 1984–1985 miners' dispute. The workforce waged a highly effective campaign, echoing the slogans of the Upper Clyde Shipbuilders and identifying the Conservative Party as pursuing a deliberate policy of deindustrialisation.[14]

The occupation was maintained for 101 days. The lead union was the AEUW, whose British leadership was less than enthusiastic. However, this was partially made up for by Ron Todd's pledge of support at the very start and the refusal of TGWU dockers at Grangemouth and drivers at the Partick depot in Glasgow to handle any Caterpillar materials.[15] Initially, the stewards were successful in repelling legal challenges in the courts – although eventually an appeal by the Caterpillar executives saw Scots case law amended and, in face of a constant media assault and new offers of redundancy, the occupation was ended. Nonetheless, for the Conservative Party, the damage had been done. In the subsequent general election, the Scottish Conservatives suffered their worst ever defeat – in stark contrast to England.

Deindustrialisation, Tory Politics and Community Mobilisation

Deindustrialisation had now become the key issue. The constant closure of major firms, including British Leyland Bathgate, which finally shut in 1986, now highlighted deindustrialisation as an integral and deliberate element of Conservative policy.[16] The Ridley Report of 1977, widely publicised during the miners' dispute, exposed the long-term Tory plans to cut back or close industries with large-scale unionised workforces – exploiting the

14 Alastair McNeill, '30 Years On: Anniversary of the Caterpillar Factory Sit-in That Lasted 103 Days', *Daily Record*, 14 January 2017.
15 Charles Woolfson, *Track Record: The Story of the Caterpillar Occupation* (Verso, 1988), pp.108 and 278.
16 Catriona Macdonald, 'The Shopfloor Experience of Regional Policy: Work and Industrial Relations at the Bathgate Motor Plant, *c.*1961–1986', PhD thesis, Glasgow University, 2013.

pound's new status as a petrocurrency to export capital – and then later to reconstruct the country's industrial base with new smaller-scale 'sunrise' non-union plants.[17] And while this motivation was as much political as economic, the temporary conversion of the pound into a high-value petrocurrency was probably the major reason why US corporations chose their British plants for closure within their global restructuring plans. And Scotland's economy, with its disproportionate levels of external corporate investment, suffered particularly badly.[18]

Equally, the overvalued petrocurrency pound disadvantaged all locally based firms – as TGWU organiser John Taylor found in the north-east's textile industry. Over this period, almost all the traditional producers were closed. The strong pound penalised exports, cheapened competing imports and choked off new local investment. Ludlows, Richards, Crombies, among other traditional north-east textile firms, all went out of business. By the 1990s, just one local firm, Johnstons of Elgin, survived – the only one to have continued investing.[19] A similar pattern of cheap imports and minimal local investment also decimated textiles in the Borders.

As we will see, immediately after the 1987 election, the question of a Scottish parliament, with industrial policy powers, was once more raised by a new civic movement led by the STUC, in which the TGWU, under its new regional secretary Willie Queen, played a significant part. Before then, however, it is important to record the TGWU's role in two other solidarity actions, those in support of the miners and the print workers, and more generally in sustaining wider support within working-class communities.

The TGWU was the one union that at a British level made a significant financial subvention to the NUM during the strike.[20] As elsewhere, members of the TGWU, at branch, workplace and community levels, provided both financial and physical support. TGWU executive member Jane McKay collected tens of thousands of pounds through the Glasgow Trades Council and its network of community collections. Similar support came from all urban centres. In Dundee, as convener of the giant Michelin factory, John Taylor ensured weekly collections and the 'adoption' of miners' children across the Tay in the Fife coalfield.[21]

17   This is examined by Charles Woolfson, John Foster and Matthais Beck, in *Paying for the Piper: Capital and Labour in Britain's Offshore Oil Industry* (Routledge, 1977), pp.33–34, citing articles in favour of fast extraction (and temporary deindustrialisation) in the *Daily Telegraph* (9 June 1976 and 7 July 1977) and against fast extraction in *The Economist* (15 January 1978 and 27 May 1978).

18   Boyle, *Scotland's Economy*, pp.5–7.

19   Tommy Campbell interview with John Taylor, September 2021 (interview 1), Unite archive, Holborn.

20   Seumas Milne, *The Enemy Within: The Secret War against the Miners* (Verso, 2014), p.154.

21   Tommy Campbell, interview 1.

In Scotland, because of the local authority control of police, there was, it appears, an initial reluctance to adopt the same tactics as in England. The 2020 Independent Report by the Scottish Parliament found some evidence that it required personal intervention by Mrs Thatcher as prime minister on 8 May 1984 to bring a change of attitude. Within two days, by 10 May, police forces were actively blockading key transport points.[22] TGWU member Jackson Cullinane remembers being halted by police on his way to deliver food, cash collections and supplies to miners' pickets at Hunterston – the key coal supply port for the Ravenscraig steel works.[23] Subsequently, action by Scottish courts, particularly in Ayrshire, resulted in significantly higher levels of convictions (and consequent dismissals) compared with English courts. Throughout the strike, the transport of imported coal remained a key issue, and it is clear from *The Highway* that in England some TGWU members, under pressure from employers, did break picket lines against instructions from the union.[24] It is unclear how far, in Scotland, this was an issue. Significantly, in Scotland, a non-union transport operator, Yuill & Dodds, had been established in the run-up to the strike, specifically for the purpose of maintaining coal deliveries.

A year later, similar challenges were experienced in March 1986 when Rupert Murdoch locked out his print workers. Murdoch's new printing base in Glasgow was a warehouse in Kinning Park, where TNT lorries, the non-union company used by Murdoch to distribute his papers, faced nightly blockades by print workers and supporting trade unions. Jackson Cullinane, by then convener at ICI's Ardeer plant, remembers regularly joining the picket with others from the wider trade union movement. Norman King, at that time a SOGAT member working in Aberdeen, made the 100-mile journey a couple of times in coaches organised by the Trades Council and the union. He recalls the scale of solidarity. Banners from across the Scottish trade union movement were on display: the UCS stewards, TGWU, NUPE, NALGO, NUJ, CPSA, AEU and TASS, as well as the print unions themselves.[25]

These movements of solidarity were in part sustained by a network of unemployed workers' centres that by the mid-1980s were spread across Scotland, mostly established by local Trades Councils and trade unions. Of these unions the most significant was the TGWU. The centres were not overtly political. But those who used them often were – having suffered job

22 Scottish Government, 'Policing of the Miners' Strike 1984–1985 – Impact on Communities: Independent Review', 28 October 2020. www.gov.scot/publications/independent-review-impact-communities-policing-miners-strike-1984-85/.
23 Interview with Jackson Cullinane, 28 April 2021, Unite Oral History Archive.
24 *The Highway*, May 1984, p.2, August 1984, p.1, November 1984, p.1.
25 Jackson Cullinane, interview, 28 April 2021; Norman King, interview 10 March 2022, Unite Oral History Archive.

loss in the highly politicised circumstances of the 1980s and having learned the lessons of the need for organisation and solidarity. These users were also often women. In the Aberdeen centre, Tommy Campbell, development officer from 1985 and bringing with him experience of community organising from Belfast, developed a new awareness of the traditions of working-class history and of the creative talents of the users themselves.[26] Similarly, in Edinburgh, another TGWU member, Pat Stuart, developed self-help groups among women focused on campaigning on equalities and occupational health at the trade union-based Lothians Community Resource Centre. So also did the network of centres across the Glasgow area run by Jane McKay from Glasgow Trades Council.

These developments were important in themselves, creating a new level of community-based organisation, often led by women, which had explicit links with the trade union and labour movement. But they proved particularly important in 1987–1988, when the Scottish Office under Rifkind, now with virtually no democratic mandate, decided to use Scotland as a test case for the introduction of a poll tax.

The poll tax bore down particularly heavily on working-class households and especially on those with adult offspring, employed or not. The level of the resulting civil disobedience was unprecedented – with, as Jackson Cullinane remembers in Ayrshire, registrations' officers being driven out of local working-class communities. In Aberdeen, Tommy Campbell recalls people massing in the housing schemes to stop sheriff officers auctioning off possessions. Women again were to the fore. Attempts at legal enforcement were seen collectively as attacks on the wider community.

This emergence of women to the leadership of the resistance was in part the result of wider socio-economic factors. Deindustrialisation and mass unemployment increasingly made women the main bread winners as well as organisers of mutual support. The steadily increasing proportion of women within union membership reflects this wider trend. But there was also an element of leadership – particularly within the TGWU. Here three women in particular (and jointly) took the lead. There was Jane McKay, by then a TGWU executive member, Yvonne Strachan, appointed first women's officer for Scotland in 1983, and Maria Fyfe, the TGWU-sponsored MP for Glasgow Maryhill. Hugh Wyper, as regional secretary, can also be credited with having facilitated these developments. In turn, Jane McKay and Yvonne Strachan worked with Ronnie McDonald, assistant general secretary at the STUC, to generalise the new women's agenda across the trade union movement – a role later picked up by Pat Stuart when she became a TGWU executive member in 1997.[27]

26 Interview with Tommy Campbell, 15 July 2021, Unite Oral History Archive.
27 Yvonne Strachan, interviews 20 and 26 November 2020, Unite Oral History Archive.

The Renewed Movement for a Scottish Parliament

It was in this context of mobilised working-class communities with women often the key organisers that a renewed movement emerged for a Scottish parliament. This came after the Conservative Party had gone down to massive defeat in Scotland in the 1987 election but then immediately and consequentially, under direct pressure from Margaret Thatcher, began a new and very conscious drive to undermine the class cohesion of working-class communities in Scotland.[28] The revived movement for a Scottish parliament consequently had a significantly different character to that in 1977–1978: less institutional, more committed to equalities and the representation of a diversity of communities. Building on the work of the Campaign for a Scottish Assembly formed in 1980, the 1988 election saw the emergence of the Claim of Right drafted by John Ross and Canon Kenyon Wright in 1989 and then the Scottish Constitutional Convention – a body designed to represent this diversity. The Convention sought to build a consensus involving churches, local government, business, political parties and the voluntary sector – but much of its political weight and momentum came from the STUC, then probably at the peak of its influence.

'There has,' wrote Professor James Kellas, 'never been a Convention with such a wide membership, and with such an extended series of meetings.'[29] Many of its recommendations were indeed carried forward into the 1998 Act which established the Scottish Parliament. Yvonne Strachan, as a trade union member of the Scottish Convention of Women, represented it on the Convention Executive. She saw it as drawing on the first Scottish Assembly convened by the STUC in 1972 but going much further in vision and aspiration. It sought to found the basis for a new democracy in Scotland as truly responsive to its people and with the potential to make radical changes such as equal representation. It sought to encompass the progressive aspirations of a broad alliance that quite explicitly saw itself as resisting an externally imposed neoliberal regime. It did so, moreover, in 1988, at the very point when Scotland witnessed neoliberalism's most brutal and blatant consequences.

On the evening of 6 July 1988, the Piper Alpha oil rig caught fire – burning through the night and killing 167 crew members. The Public Inquiry, chaired by Lord Cullen, lasted from January 1989 to February 1990 and heard 266 witnesses. Its findings explicitly linked the disaster

28 Chik Collins, *Language, Ideology and Consciousness: Developing a Sociohistorical Approach* (Routledge, 1999), details the exchange between Thatcher and Rifkind that drove the new 'urban policy' of direct intervention in working-class communities.
29 James Kellas, 'The Scottish Constitutional Convention', *Scottish Government Year Book 1992* (Edinburgh University Press, 1992); Lindsay Paterson, *A Diverse Assembly: The Debate on a Scottish Parliament* (Edinburgh University Press, 1998).

to the organisation of Britain's offshore oil and gas and the extraction regime it imposed on workers: the initial deal with the United States in 1971–1973 for ultrafast development, the consequent implantation of a US management regime (directly run by US subcontractors), the virtual exclusion of trade union organisation and the shocking exemption of the UK sector (largely at the behest of the US operators) from the provisions of the 1974 Health and Safety at Work Act. All this was exposed at the hearings of the Cullen Inquiry. The exposure was made even more shocking by the contrast with the immediately adjacent Norwegian sector. Here, in an industry with far better health and safety statistics, trade unions were recognised and health and safety provisions enforced – within a production regime that required the use of local suppliers, enforced long-term depletion controls and was owned by a state company, Statoil. Equally, the immediate causes of Piper Alpha were exposed as consequences of the policies of the Thatcher government itself – its initial reliance on (and exploitation of) sky-high oil prices, its inadequate response to their collapse in 1984–1986, the consequent laying off of 20 per cent of the workforce and, as a result, the virtual abandonment of rig maintenance.[30]

Tommy Campbell remembers the trauma in Aberdeen and further afield. Many of the workers on the rigs were recruited from the now decimated industrial communities of Scotland's central belt and the ex-mining areas. Scarcely a town or village was without a death to mourn. The Aberdeen Unemployed Workers' Centre became the focus for individual contact and support.[31]

It was also as a consequence of the Piper Alpha disaster, of the resulting mobilisation of off-shore workers and of the loss of authority by the oil-operating companies that the Oil Industry Liaison Committee was formed in February 1989, originally at the initiative of the TGWU, AEUW and NUS, to develop a united campaign for trade union represen-tation.[32] The TGWU, led by its regional officer, John Taylor, had previously managed to establish a relatively strong organisation among catering workers, notably including women, and possessed a network of over 70 shop stewards on all rigs across the UK sector. In 1990, almost exactly two years after Piper Alpha, but before the safety recommendations of the Cullen Inquiry had been implemented, six more rig workers were killed in the Sikorsky helicopter crash. That summer, with the first Iraq war pushing oil prices back to record levels, saw the first of the 24-hour sit-in strikes across the UK sector of the North Sea.

30 Woolfson and Beck, *Paying for the Piper*, pp.39–41 and 301 ff.
31 Interview with Tommy Campbell, July 2021, Unite Oral History Archive.
32 Tommy Campbell interview with John Taylor, September 2021 (interview 2), Unite Oral History Archive.

Scotland, therefore, had a particularly direct and explicit encounter with Thatcherite neoliberalism and its assault on working people. The TGWU, as the country's biggest union, played a key part in mobilising resistance and in supporting demands for a Scottish parliament – specifically as an institution that would embody the aspirations of working people. The following years did indeed reveal a somewhat different outcome. But key expectations and commitments had been established.

10

Postscript: The TGWU into the 1990s

As we have seen, the 1980s witnessed a decade of decline for the trade union movement, especially for those unions like the TGWU which organised primarily in the manufacturing sector. Changes to union density, the decline of collective bargaining and centrally negotiated agreements, all underpinned by anti-union legislation, marked a fundamental reversal since the heady days of the 1970s. The anti-union laws of the Conservative governments of this period succeeded, as intended, to shift the balance of power between labour and capital decisively in favour of capital.

The final years of Ron Todd's tenure as general secretary witnessed even greater retrenchment within the TGWU as it struggled to cope with declining membership and a succession of industrial defeats. The BDC of 1991 marked a new phase in the process of cost-cutting. Todd presented the GEC statement on finance, which announced bluntly that the expenditure of the union had now exceeded membership income. Accordingly, Bill Morris, deputy general secretary, presented a somewhat unpopular programme of cuts to withstand the deficit. This was based on the proposals of a special working party, the terms of reference of which were 'to draft a financial strategy to resolve the current deficit situation of the union, and to review the organisation of the union and make recommendations'.[1]

These recommendations included a reduction in full-time officers and staff through a programme of early retirement and the closure of many regional and local offices. The report stated that union offices should be closed in areas where there had been major decline in manufacturing or traditional employment and should be located only in those places 'in which there is industrial logic'.[2] Thus far, it was reported, 22 offices had

1 Quoted in John Fisher, *Bread on the Waters: A History of TGWU Education 1922–2000* (Lawrence & Wishart, 2005), p.254.
2 Verbatim minutes, 1991 TGWU BDC, Unite archive, Holborn.

been closed or were under review, but 13 offices had been opened 'to service a large potential membership'.[3] Nonetheless, branch administration was to be reduced by 2.5 per cent. Although no figure was set for Central Office expenditure, the conference was informed that this was under 'close review' and that a 'more rigorous systems of cost control and financial planning' would be introduced.[4]

Following this report, regions offered their response to it. Some had already begun a process of retrenchment, but others were highly critical of the GEC statement, arguing that little had been done centrally to offset spiralling expenditure, and that branches and members had borne the cost of retrenchment while central office itself was profligate.

Despite reservations, these plans for retrenchment involving not only deep budget cuts but also major structural reorganisation were implemented following the GEC's agreement to commission a report by an American organisational consultant, Adam Klein. His report and its outcome will be dealt with more fully in the next volume of this history (*Unite History*, volume 6).

The other tried and tested strategy for reversing decline was to increase membership by merging with other unions. Merger and amalgamation was nothing new for the TGWU – indeed, as a general union, its very foundation in 1922 was accomplished by the amalgamation of 22 unions and many others subsequently, although most of these were not necessitated purely through the predicament of falling membership income. The resulting outcome of pre-existing mergers was the unique trade group structure of the TGWU. It was this multi-trade group structure that, according to Bill Morris, made the union 'ideally suited to mergers and transfers of engagements'.[5] On this basis, he introduced the new phase of the 'merger strategy' at the 1991 BDC – a strategy primarily based on an attempt to resolve the ongoing financial crisis. The eventual outcome of this strategy was the merger process which resulted in the creation of Unite the Union in 2007. This will be fully explored in volume 6.

During this period (1974–1992), as has been noted, several successful mergers were completed, but some attempts were unsuccessful, notably with the GMB and with the NUM.[6] The merger with the NUM had originally been suggested in 1988, and was revived in 1991, despite the opposition of Jack Dromey (TGWU National Secretary for Public Services), who complained that he knew nothing about bilateral talks with the NUM and that he was already in talks with members employed by

3 Verbatim minutes, 1991 TGWU BDC.
4 Verbatim minutes, 1991 TGWU BDC.
5 Verbatim minutes, 1991 TGWU BDC.
6 MRC MSS.572/72. NUM/TGWU merger talks; see Joe Irvin's detailed paper on how the two unions would work together (18 November 1988).

British Nuclear Fuels and the Atomic Energy Authority in the hope that a new Energy trade group could be established in the TGWU.[7]

And so this volume ends on a somewhat bleak note. It has chronicled defeat and decline, alongside an ideological onslaught on trade union and socialist values emanating not only from Thatcherite neoliberal ideology, but also from within the labour movement itself in the form of the politics of 'new realism' and the 'third way'. This, together with vicious anti-trade union legislation, had a profound impact of the labour movement's ability to withstand the well-planned Tory strategy, clearly articulated in its 'Stepping Stones' programme, resulting in the promised privatisation of nationalised industries and the public sector, deindustrialisation, mass unemployment and the use of vicious state repression to defeat industrial action. Thus the TGWU along with many other unions witnessed more defeats than victories. But, throughout its history, the labour movement has shown an uncanny ability to rebuild and renew itself, with the consequence that its detractors, keen as they always are to write the movement's premature obituary, continue to be wrong-footed. Working-class organisations do not proceed in a linear, onward and upward fashion. They are always marked by peaks and troughs in activity, effectiveness and membership.

The daily battle between capital and labour continued to be waged, albeit less successfully, in altered forms and circumstances despite the legal restrictions to emasculate it. Undoubtedly, real gains within the TGWU and other unions were made for women and black members. Indeed, the broader issue of equality for under-represented or marginalised groups had at last made a belated appearance on the agenda of the union.

The history of the labour movement has always been halting and problematic – this was certainly the case in this period. These ups and downs are not always crudely determined by economic circumstances but have a great deal to do with the prevailing level of understanding that the essence of trade unionism is the struggle between capital and labour. The fact that this elusive construct escapes causal explanation does not invalidate its existence. At key moments, its presence determines the defiant rather than the defensive aspect of the movement when it consciously seeks to fight back in order to challenge exploitation and oppression. Variously, the ideologies inspiring these visions and the practices which they motivated could be called, in their pure and most polarised forms, left or right, radical or reactionary, socialist or capitalist, revolutionary or reformist. Rarely are the complex battles which shape a movement played out in their starkest forms, but, nonetheless, the underlying tension is there. Such battles were clearly evident in the TGWU in this period and

---

7   MRC MSS.572/72. NUM/TGWU merger talks, memo from Dromey (3 December 1991).

shaped its capacity to withstand, for better or worse, the determination of the employing class, supported by its state, to maintain and extend its power.

Index

Page numbers in **bold** refer to figures.